SISTERS OF CHARITY,

CATHOLIC AND PROTESTANT.

AND

THE COMMUNION OF LABOR.

BY

MRS. JAMESON.

BOSTON:
TICKNOR AND FIELDS.
M DCCC LVII.

Published in 1857 by Ticknor and Fields, Boston
Hyperion reprint edition 1976
Reproduced from a copy in the collection of the University of California,
Berkeley, Library
Library of Congress Catalog Number 75-15087
ISBN 0-88355-268-X
Printed in the United States of America

Library of Congress Cataloging in Publication Data

Jameson, Anna Brownell Murphy, 1794-1860.
    Sisters of charity, Catholic and Protestant and
The communion of labor.

    (Pioneers of the woman's movement ; 8)
    ~~*Reprint of the 1857 ed. published by Ticknor and*~~
~~*Fields, Boston.*~~
        1. Sisters of Charity — Addresses, essays, lectures.
2. Women in charitable work — Addresses, essays, lectures.
3. Nursing — Moral and religious aspects — Addresses, essays,
lectures. I. Jameson, Anna Brownell Murphy, 1794-1860.
The communion of labor. 1976. II. Title.
BX4237.J35   1976   271'.9'1   75-15087
ISBN 0-88355-268-X

FLORENCE NIGHTINGALE.

IF on this verse of mine
Those eyes shall ever shine,
Whereto sore-wounded men have looked for life,
Think not that for a rhyme,
Nor yet to fit the time,
I name thy name, — true victress in this strife !
But let it serve to say
That, when we kneel to pray,
Prayers rise for thee thine ear shall never know ;
And that thy gallant deed,
For God, and for our need,
Is in all hearts, as deep as love can go.

'Tis good that thy name springs
From two of Earth's fair things, —
A stately city and a soft-voiced bird ;
'Tis well that in all homes,
When thy sweet story comes,
And brave eyes fill — that pleasant sounds be heard.
Oh voice ! in night of fear,
As night's bird, soft to hear,
Oh great heart ! raised like city on a hill ;
Oh watcher ! worn and pale,
Good Florence Nightingale,
Thanks, loving thanks, for thy large work and will !
England is glad of thee, —
Christ for thy charity,
Take thee to joy when hand and heart are still !

EDWIN ARNOLD.

SISTERS OF CHARITY,

CATHOLIC AND PROTESTANT,

ABROAD AND AT HOME.

" It is manifest that all the human material which Christian endeavors may be able to mould into order and usefulness, will be required for the growing exigencies of the state." — Rev. Mr. CLAY. (*Report on the Preston Jail*, 1852.)

PREFACE.

WHEN the following Lecture was delivered, on the 28th of last June, more than one half was omitted, in consequence of its too great length. The idea of dividing it into two separate Lectures was abandoned, for reasons which it is unnecessary to state here. It is now printed as it was originally written, with some additional notes and details. It must be considered, on the whole, as merely supplementary to the Lecture on " Sisters of Charity," published last year; as an illustration and expansion, through facts and examples, of the principles there briefly set forth,—namely, that a more equal distribution of the work which has to be done, and a more perfect communion of interests in the work which is done, are,

which almost every post has brought to me from medical men, from clergymen, from intelligent women, (the greater number strangers to me personally,) either expressive of cordial sympathy, or conveying practical suggestions, or offering aid and co-operation; — all, however various the contents, testifying to the great truths I have endeavored to illustrate in these pages: namely, that there exists at the core of our social condition a great mistake to be corrected, and a great want supplied; that men and women must learn to understand each other, and work together for the common good, before any amount of permanent moral and religious progress can be effected; and that, in the most comprehensive sense of the word, we need Sisters of Charity everywhere.

In some few of these letters a tone of expostulation mingles with that of kind approval; and my attention is directed to various institutions which exist at present as filling up the want I have pointed out; — for instance, the efficiency of some of the Normal schools for the preparation of female teachers, and the encouragement which has been given to the houses recently established for training sick nurses, are especially dwelt upon. I learn that one of our most distinguished men entertains

the project of organizing " classes " for work-
ingwomen, as he has already aided in elevating
the mental and moral standard for the working-
men. Again, there are hopes that, in spite of
all opposing influences, lessons in elementary
physiology will be more generally introduced
into schools. God forbid that we should be
insensible to the efforts which have been made,
and are extending in all directions, for the
amelioration of crying social evils! But what
we require is not more benevolence, but the
general recognition of sounder and larger principles than have hitherto directed that benevolence. With all our schools of all denomi-
nations, it remains an astounding fact, that
one half of the women who annually become
wives in this England of ours cannot sign
their names in the parish register; that this
amount of ignorance in the lower classes is
accompanied by an amount of ill health, despondency, inaptitude, and uselessness in the
so-called " educated classes;" which, taken
together, prove that our boasted appliances
are, to a great extent, failures.

And, first, with regard to the means afforded
for training nurses for the sick. I would ask
what is the number of women so trained?
Does it amount to one in every five hundred
thousand of our female population? Does it

amount to one hundred altogether? and for
whose service are these women trained? Are
they distributed among our village poor, our
country infirmaries? Up to a very recent
period, till the need of nurses for the East
excited public attention, were not the greater
number of these trained nurses in the service of the rich? What is done is well done,
perhaps; let us be thankful it is done; but
is it sufficient? Does it meet those wants in
the community which I have ventured to point
out in the pages which follow?

Go into yon spacious hospital, provided with
all that wealth, and skill, and knowledge can
combine to heal or to ameliorate bodily suffering: see the floors how clean, the linen how
spotless, the beds how comfortable! the most
celebrated of our surgeons and physicians are
in attendance; students from every part of
England crowd thither;— it is one of the best
of our medical schools. Let us approach a bed;
— it is a poor pale girl, dying of a slow decline; she has been stretched there for eleven
months; the chaplain duly visits her once or
twice a week in her turn, for he has about
five hundred other human souls to attend to.
The physician, as he goes his rounds, pats
her on the head; asks her, in a tone of unusual pity, the usual questions; then, perhaps,

turns to two or three students who follow him, and almost aloud expresses his wonder to find her still alive. The nurse duly administers the prescription, and on pain of dismissal sees that every want is attended to. Is nothing else needed ? Is anything else supplied ? A melancholy religious tract, perhaps : but for the spontaneous action of mind upon mind, — for tender, human, sympathizing love, — for help to the sinking spirit, — where are they ? It is no answer to appeal to individual cases ; to cite one or two hospitals, in which thoughtful and kindly women of the higher classes have been permitted to visit; — in which the superior intellect and administrative faculties of the matron for the time being have exercised an improving influence. These are the exceptions ; and until larger, higher principles of action are generally recognized, they will continue to be *accidental* exceptions to the prevalence of a narrow-minded mechanical system.

In several of the letters I have received, the condition of some of our workhouses, in town and country, is set forth at length : and surely it is worth considering whether the administration of these institutions might not be improved by the aid of kindly and intelligent women sharing with the overseers the task of supervision. The most conscientious men are

apt to treat the wretched paupers as if they
had neither hearts to be touched, nor souls to
be saved. The paid matrons are taken from
a class scarcely a grade above them ; often as
ignorant, as miserable, as debased as themselves, and wholly unfit to be intrusted with
power. Do the aged, while swallowing per-
force the dregs of a bitter life, find any reverence, any pity ? Do the children, — poor little
scraps of a despised humanity, — find tenderness, freedom, or cheerfulness ? Can any one
doubt that the element of power disunited
from the element of Christian love must in
the long run become a hard, cold, cruel machine ? and that this must *of necessity* be the
result where the masculine energy acts independent of the feminine sympathies ? The
men who manage in their own way these
abodes of destitution, dread, not without some
reason, any troublesome interference with established routine through the intervention of
impulsive womanly instincts, which, ill-trained,
misdirected, and unenlightened, may do mischief; but must they, therefore, be set wholly
aside ? How long shall this absurd and unmanly jealousy in one class of men, — the men
who fill public or municipal offices, — be
allowed to petrify the public heart, and cripple
the means of doing good? How long shall

the narrow prejudices of another class of men,
— the husbands, brothers, and fathers, — withhold women from a sphere of healthy action,
and thus perpetuate and widen the gulf which
separates class from class ?

The principle kept in view by the Poor Law
guardians and overseers is to save the money
of the parish, — a very proper and honorable
principle in those who have to administer it; —
but is not a wiser and more beneficent expen-
diture of the parish rates possible ? Some of
those who are largely taxed to pay those rates
think so. Since it is allowed on all hands
that we want Institutions for the training of
efficient " Sisters of Charity " for all offices
connected with the sick, the indigent, the
fallen, and the ignorant among us, why should
not our parish workhouses be made available
for the purpose ? In such an application of
means and funds already at hand, it appears
to me that there would be both good sense
and economy, therefore it ought to recommend
itself to our so-called practical men.

I remember when, some years ago, the first
trial was made at Birmingham to institute
what has since been called " Schools for the
Adult Females employed in the Manufac-
tories." The Legislature had restricted the
hours of labor, and the women, when dis-

missed from work, shrunk into lonely, dirty,
neglected homes, or walked the streets, or congregated into the vilest public-houses. They
earned good wages, yet hardly one in ten
could read or write; they were ignorant of
any feminine or household work; they were
dirty, reckless, wasteful; unsexed, if not un-
chaste. Some ladies, true " Sisters of Charity," united to open a refuge where these
women could obtain light and warmth without the temptation of drink and bad company,
and the means of instruction if they were so
minded, although it was not forced upon them.
Will it be believed that every possible difficulty and obstacle was thrown in the way of
this project by masters and overseers? —
Those who undertook the work of mercy, and
at length carried it out, had to conquer the
ground occupied by masculine prejudices inch
by inch; and now it is among the women they
have rescued that the employers seek their
steadiest female " hands," that the workmen
look for tidy, good tempered wives.

Another point to which my attention has
been drawn, and which has an especial interest
at present, is the condition of the soldiers'
wives. I hardly dare to describe the state of
things which has been allowed to exist in the
barracks and military depôts up to the present

time; — from six to sixteen married couples
sleeping together in one room, and in some
instances unmarried girls, daughters of the
soldiers, living among them, and brought up
in this human stye! When a woman of
decent habits is introduced to such a scene,
can we wonder that in a few weeks she should
become a mere female beast, or learn to drown
in drink the unutterable misery and degradation of her position? Who are the " officers
and gentlemen" who honor their mothers,
who guard with such care the delicacy of their
wives and daughters, yet can expose women
to ignominy like this? If the wives of these
" officers and gentlemen" were expected, as a
matter of duty, incident to their social position, or, at least, were allowed by their husbands, to take an interest in the well-being of
the soldiers and their wives, could these things
have existed? Is it not matter of astonishment and humiliation among us that the expediency of giving decent lodging to the married
men is only now discussed by the military
authorities? I would suggest that the well-
educated, and benevolent, and energetic women married to officers in command, should
take counsel with their husbands on the possibility of organizing into an efficient working
staff the women who belong to each regiment.

Instead of only the most depraved and worthless women being allowed to inhabit the barracks, these should be turned out, while the
most respectable should be retained and
classed according to their capabilities ; some
as teachers of the children ; some as nurses
of the sick ; others as sempstresses to mend
and take care of the linen ; others as washerwomen.   What sort of creatures are those
who have gone to the East with our army ? —
Are they not a despair, a disgrace to our authorities, — as utterly uselses as they are
utterly worthless ?   We have now the spirit
of a noble womanhood, roused up at home
and at a distance, to remedy these evils ; but
had it been earlier roused, and earlier used
and appreciated, such evils never could have
existed.

I must conclude by thanking my correspon-
dents generally for the approbation which has
cheered, and the sympathy which has comforted.   Considerations of health take me far
away from England for the present; but on
my return I hope to find kindly and active
spirits and wise heads doing the practical
work which I cannot do myself.   It has been
said that we need some protest against the
tendency of this age to deify mere material
power, mere mechanism, mere intellect, and

what is called the " philosophy of the *positif.*"
It appears to me that God's good providence
is preparing such a counterpoise in the more
equal and natural apportioning of the work
that is to be done on earth ; in the due min-
gling of the softer charities and purer moral
discipline of the home life with all the material
interests of social and political life ; in the
better training of the affectionate instincts of
the woman's nature, and the application of
these to purposes and objects which have hitherto been considered as out of their province
or beyond their reach ; for what can concern
the community at large which does not concern women also ?

May 1, 1855.

PREFACE

TO THE FIRST EDITION.

I HAVE been induced to publish this little
Lecture in its present form, because it places
some of the questions which are now promi-
nently before the public on grounds which,
if not new, are at least not generally admitted,
still less advocated. The results of a large
amount of private information and of personal observation are here condensed into the
smallest possible compass. I have also used
unhesitatingly all the published material at
hand, from which I could extract either
thought, or fact, available for my purpose.
I must especially acknowledge my obligations
to a little book, entitled " Hospitals and
Sisterhoods " (published by Murray) ; to a
small pamphlet, entitled " Kaiserswerth on the
Rhine " (published by Hookham) ; and to the

Reports of the last named Institution placed in my hands some time ago. Other authorities are referred to in the notes, but I could not certify all. In fact, the following pages contain the spirit — *quintessencié* — of my experience, observation, and reading, on the education and employments of women for many years past.

The subject has suddenly taken a form which appeals to popular sympathies. Names and deeds have, of late, been sounded through the brazen trumpet of publicity, and mixed up, unhappily, with party and sectarian discord, which ought rather to have been whispered tenderly and reverentially in our prayers; but since it is so, and cannot now be helped, I have not hesitated to allude to persons and to circumstances which, I trust, are not the less dear because they have become in some sort public property, nor the less sacred, because they have become celebrated.

I have received since this Lecture was delivered, or rather *read*, many communications, either expressive of sympathy or illustrating by additional facts the arguments which are here very summarily and unmethodically brought together. I cannot despair of the practical result, however distant it may seem; nor can I look round me without being "transported beyond this ignorant present" into that wiser future, which I as confidently anticipate, as I truly believe in the goodness and all-ruling providence of God.

A. J.

March 26, 1855.

SISTERS OF CHARITY,

ABROAD AND AT HOME.

A LECTURE

(Delivered privately February 14th, 1855, and printed by desire).

————

MY FRIENDS: — The subject on which I venture to address you is one which will find an interest in every kind heart. It is also one of incalculable social importance. I am to discourse to you of SISTERS OF CHARITY, not merely as the designation of a particular order of religious women, belonging to a particular church, but also in a far more comprehensive sense, as indicating the vocation of a large number of women in every country, class, and creed. I wish to point out to you what has been done in other countries, and may be done in ours, to make this vocation available for public uses and for social progress.

I have to beg your patience, — your indulgence. It will be necessary for me to advert
to subjects on which there exists considerable
difference of opinion; while the brevity required by a lecture will not allow me to discuss these at length, or to submit all the arguments which might be advanced in favor of
my own convictions. I am obliged to con-
centrate what I have to say into the smallest
possible compass; nevertheless, by recurring
to first principles, instead of discussing ways
and means, and questions of expediency, I
think I shall facilitate the object in view.
The deeper we can lay our foundation, the
safer will be our superstructure. Therefore,
to begin at the beginning: —

There are many different theories concerning the moral purposes of this world in which
we dwell, considered, I mean, in reference to
us, its human inhabitants; for some regard it
merely as a state of transition between two
conditions of existence, a past and a future;
others as being worthless in itself, except as a
probation or preparation for a better and a

higher life; while others, absorbed or saddened by the monstrous evils and sorrows around them, have really come to regard it as a place of punishment or penance for sins committed in a former state of existence. But I think that the best definition, — the best, at least, for our present purpose, — is that of Shakspeare: he calls it, with his usual felicity of expression, "*this working-day world;*" and it is truly this: it is a place where work is to be done, — work which *must* be done, — work which it is *good* to do; — a place in which labor of one kind or another is at once the condition of existence and the condition of happiness.

Well, then, in this working-day world of ours we must all work. The only question is, what shall we do? To few is it granted to choose their work. Indeed, all work worth the doing seems to leave us no choice. We are called to it. Sometimes the voice so calling is from within, sometimes from without; but in any case it is what we term expressively our *vocation*, and in either case the harmony

and happiness of life in man or woman consists in finding in our vocation the employment of our highest faculties, and of as many
of them as can be brought into action.

And work is of various kinds: there are
works of necessity and works of mercy; —
head work, *hand* work; — man's work, woman's work; and on the distribution of this
work in accordance with the divine law, and
what Milton calls the " faultless proprieties
of nature," depends the well-being of the
whole community, not less than that of each
individual.

Domestic life, the acknowledged foundation
of all social life, has settled by a natural law
the work of the man and the work of the
woman. The man governs, sustains, and
defends the family; the woman cherishes,
reglulates, and purifies it; but though distinct,
the relative work is inseparable, — sometimes
exchanged, sometimes shared; so that from
the beginning, we have, even in the primitive
household, not the *division*, but the *communion*
of labor.

As civilization advances, as the social interests and occupations become more and more complicated, the family duties and influences diverge from the central home, — in a manner, radiate from it, — though it is always there in reality. The man becomes on a larger scale, father and brother, sustainer and defender; the woman becomes on a larger scale, mother and sister, nurse and help.

Of course, the relations thus multiplied and diffused are less sacred, less intense, but also less egotistical, less individual, than in the primitive tent of the Arab, the lodge of the red-man, or within the precincts of the civilized hearth; but in proportion as we can carry out socially the family duties and charities, and perform socially the household-work, just in such proportion is society safely and harmoniously constituted.

If domestic life be then the foundation and the bond of all social communities, does it not seem clear that there must exist between man and woman, even from the beginning, the

communion of love and the communion of
labor? By the first I understand all the benevolent affections and their results, and all
the binding charities of life, extended from
the home into the more ample social relations; and in the latter I comprehend all the
active duties, all intellectual exercise of the
faculties, also extended from the central home
into the larger social circle. When from the
cross those memorable words were uttered by
our Lord, "Behold thy Mother! Behold thy
Son!" do you think they were addressed only
to the two desolate mourners who then and
there wept at his feet? No, — they were
spoken, like all his words, to the wide universe, to all humanity, to all time!

I rest, therefore, all I have to say hereafter
upon what I conceive to be a great vital truth,
— an unchangeable, indisputable, natural law.
And it is this: that men and women are by
nature mutually dependent, mutually helpful;
that this communion exists not merely in one
or two relations, which custom may define
and authorize, and to which opinion may re-

strict them in this or that class, in this or that
position; but must extend to every possible
relation in existence in which the two sexes
can be socially approximated. Thus, for instance, a man, in the first place, merely sustains and defends his home; then he works to
sustain and defend the community or the
nation he belongs to: and so of woman; she
begins by being the nurse, the teacher, the
cherisher of her home, through her greater tenderness and purer moral sentiments; then she
uses these qualities and sympathies on a larger
scale, to cherish and purify society. But still
the man and the woman must continue to
share the work; there must be the communion
of labor in the large human family just as
there was within the narrower precincts of
home.

You will wonder that I begin with truisms
such as no man in his senses never thinks of
disputing; but the wonder is that, while admitted, they are never acted upon. Can you
give me any one instance in which this primal
law of our being, with regard to the distribu-

tion of work, has been taken as the natural and necessary basis for any improvement in legislation or in education? Can you point to any one among these piles of Blue-books and reports, — educational reports, sanitary reports, jail reports, juvenile delinquent reports, — in which such principles are adverted to? It is granted as a principle that ample scope should be given for the man to perform his share of the social work, and ample means of instruction to enable him to perform it well. What provision is made to enable the woman to do *her* work well and efficiently?

It is not charity, nor energy, nor intelligence which are wanting in our women, any more than dauntless bravery in our men. But something *is* wanting; or surely from so much good material, more positive and extended social benefits would arise. What *is* wanting is more moral courage, more common sense on the part of our legislators. If men were better educated they would sympathize in the necessity of giving a better education to women. They would perceive the wisdom of applying, on a large and efficient

scale, the means of health, strength, and progress which lie in the gentler capacities of the
gentler sex, — material ready at hand, as yet
wasted in desultory, often misdirected, efforts,
or perishing inert, or fermenting to evil and
despair.

Lying at the source of the mischief we
trace a great *mistake* and a great *want.*

The great mistake seems to have been that,
in all our legislation, it is taken for granted
that the woman is always protected, always
under tutelage, always within the precincts of
a home; finding there her work, her interests,
her duties, and her happiness: but is this true?
We know that it is altogether false. There
are thousands and thousands of women who
have no protection, no guide, no help, no
home; — who are absolutely driven by circumstance and necessity, if not by impulse
and inclination, to carry out into the larger
community the sympathies, the domestic instincts, the active administrative capabilities
with which God has endowed them; but

these instincts, sympathies, capabilities, require, first, to be properly developed, then properly trained, and then directed into large and useful channels, according to the individual tendencies.

As to the want, what I insist on particularly is, that the means do not exist for the training of those powers; that the sphere of duties which should occupy them is not acknowledged; and I must express my deep conviction that society is suffering in its depths through this great mistake and this great want.

We require in our country the recognition, — the public recognition, — by law as well as by opinion, of the woman's privilege to share in the communion of labor at her own free choice, and the foundation of institutions which shall train her to do her work well.

I am anxious that you should not misunderstand me at the outset with regard to this " *woman-question,*" as it has been called.   I

have no intention to discuss either the rights
or the wrongs of women. I think that on this
question our relations across the Atlantic have
gone a mile beyond the winning-post, and
brought discredit and ridicule on that just
cause which, here in England, prejudice, custom, ignorance, have in a manner crushed and
smothered up. It is in this country, beyond all
Christian countries, that what has been called,
quaintly but expressively, the " feminine element of society," considered as a power applicable in many ways to the amelioration of
many social evils, has been not only neglected,
but absolutely ignored by those who govern
us. The woman cries out for the occasion and
the means to do well her appointed and permitted work, to perform worthily her share in
the natural communion of labor. Because it
is denied to her she perishes, " and no man
layeth it to heart." *

* The soliloquy of the young girl in " Shirley " is as exquisitely true to the individual character as it is illustrative
generally of an outward state of things which shuts down the
safety-valves on the morbid feeling, until a condition of health
arising out of natural causes, and which Nature intended to
be temporary and healable, becomes chronic and permanent :
— " Nobody " (she is thinking aloud) " nobody in particu-

It is true that there is no law which forbids
the woman to use her energies; but we might
as well say that no law exists in China which
forbids a woman to take a walk into the coun-

lar is to blame, that I can see, for the state in which things
are; and I cannot tell, however much I puzzle over it, how
they are to be altered for the better; but I feel there is something wrong somewhere. I believe single women should have
more to do, — better chances of interesting and profitable occupation than they possess now; and when I speak thus, I have
no impression that I displease God by my words, that I am
either impious or impatient, irreligious or sacrilegious. My
consolation is, indeed, that God hears many a groan, and
compassionates much grief which man stops his ears against,
or frowns on with impotent contempt. I say *impotent*, for I
observe that to such grievances as society cannot readily cure
it usually forbids utterance, on pain of its scorn; this scorn
being only a sort of tinselled cloak to its deformed weakness.
People hate to be reminded of ills they are unable or unwil-
ling to remedy; such reminder, in forcing on them a sense of
their own incapacity, or a more painful sense of an obligation
to make some unpleasant effort, troubles their ease and shakes
their self-complacency. Old maids, like the houseless and
unemployed poor, should not ask for a place and an occupation in the world; the demand disturbs the happy and
rich; it disturbs parents. Look at the numerous families of
girls in this neighborhood, — the Armitages, the Birtwhistles,
the Sykes. The brothers of these girls are every one in business or in professions; they have something to do : their sisters have no earthly employment but household work and
sewing; no earthly pleasure but an unprofitable visiting; and
no hope, in all their life to come, of any thing better. This
stagnant state of things makes them decline in health; they
are never well, and their minds and views shrink to wondrous

try. The Chinese content themselves with bandaging and crippling the feet of their women, which is found, as a preventive, quite as effectual as any law. In a very entertain-

narrowness. The great wish, the sole aim, of every one of them is to be married; but the majority will never marry: they will die as they now live. They scheme, they plot, they dress to ensnare husbands. The gentlemen turn them into ridicule; they don't want them; they hold them very cheap; they say, — I have heard them say it with sneering laughs many a time, — the matrimonial market is overstocked. Fathers say so likewise, and are angry with their daughters when they observe their manœuvres; they order them to stay at home. What do they expect them to do at home? If you ask, they would answer, sew and cook. They expect them to do this, and this only, contentedly, regularly, uncomplainingly, all their lives long, as if they had no germs of faculties for any thing else; — a doctrine as reasonable to hold as it would be that the fathers have no faculties but for eating what their daughters cook, or for wearing what they sew. Could men live so themselves? would they not be very weary? and when there came no relief to their weariness but only reproaches at its slightest manifestation, would not their weariness ferment in time to frenzy? Lucretia, spinning at midnight in the midst of her maidens, and Solomon's virtuous woman, are often quoted as patterns of what 'the sex' (as they say) ought to be. I don't know: Lucretia, I dare say, was a most worthy sort of person, but she kept her servants up very late. I should not have liked to be amongst the number of the maidens. The 'virtuous woman,' again, had her household up in the very middle of the night. She 'got breakfast over' before one o'clock, A. M.; but *she* had something more to do than spin and give out portions. She was a manufacturer; she made fine linen and sold it.

ing book about China, which has lately appeared, the author, M. Huc, describes some Chinese ladies setting off on a pilgrimage. Hobbling on their cramped feet, and support-

She was an agriculturist; she bought estates and planted vineyards. *That* woman was a manager. She was what the matrons hereabouts call ' a clever woman.' On the whole, I like her a good deal better than Lucretia; but I don't believe either Mr. Armitage or Mr. Sykes could have got the advantage of her in a bargain; yet I like her :— ' Strength and honor were her clothing. The heart of her husband safely trusted in her. She opened her mouth with wisdom; in her tongue was the law of kindness; her children rose up and called her blessed; her husband also praised her.' King of Israel ! your model of a woman is a worthy model ! But are we, in these days, brought up to be like her ? Men of England ! do your daughters reach this royal standard ? Can they reach it ? Can you help them to reach it ? Can you give them a field in which their faculties may be exercised and grow ? Men of England! look at your poor girls, many of them fading around you, dropping off in consumption or decline; or, what is worse, degenerating to sour old maids, — envious, backbiting, wretched, because life is a desert to them; or, what is worst of all, reduced to strive, by scarce modest coquetry and debasing artifice, to gain that position and consideration by marriage which to celibacy is denied. Fathers! cannot you alter these things ? Perhaps not all at once; but consider the matter well when it is brought before you : receive it as a theme worthy of thought; do not dismiss it with an idle jest or an unmanly insult. You would wish to be proud of your daughters, and not to blush for them. Then seek for them an interest and an occupation which shall raise them above the flirt, the manœuvrer, the mischief-making tale-bearer. Keep your girls' minds narrow and fettered,

ing themselves with a stick, they reach at last the temple to which they are bound. So it is with our women: they attain their objects; but what God made natural, graceful, and easy, is rendered matter of pain and difficulty, is regarded as an indecorum or an extravagance, and is very awkwardly and imperfectly achieved, if at all.

Now the problem which it is given to us in this age and this country to solve as well as we can, — to solve, I will say it, or perish morally, — has been partially solved by another church in other countries. And be-

— they will still be a plague and a care, sometimes a disgrace to you. Cultivate them, — give them scope and work, — they will be your gayest companions in health, your tenderest nurses in sickness, your most faithful prop in age."

I had the opportunity, on different occasions, of showing this striking passage to two clever men. One of them listened attentively, and then said, with a half-sigh, "She ought to emigrate!" The other, rather impatiently, and with a half-sneer, thus commented, — "The girl ought to be married!" Marriage and emigration have both their difficulties. And must women in this country be driven to one of these two alternatives? or resign themselves to become, as some one expresses it, the "female of the tutor or the tailor?" And this too when they are needed on every hand, in works of necessity or works of mercy?

fore I proceed to consider the subject with reference to the present condition of society and public opinion among us, let it be permitted to me to advert briefly to the institutions of charitable women, in the Roman Catholic Church, not because I think or wish that these institutions could or ought to be carried out among us precisely in the same manner, as a purely religious establishment, subservient to a hierarchy; but because I am anxious to show you the immense results of a well-organized system of work for women.

I know that many well-meaning, ignorant people in this country entertain the idea that the existence of communities of women, trained and organized to help in social work from the sentiment of devotion, is especially a Roman Catholic institution, belonging peculiarly to that church, and necessarily implying the existence of nuns and nunneries, veils and vows, forced celibacy and seclusion, and all the other inventions and traditions which, in this Protestant nation, are regarded with terror, disgust, and derision. I conceive that this is altogether a mistake. The truth seems to me to amount to this : that the Roman Catholic Church has had the good sense to turn to account, and assimilate to itself, and inform with its own peculiar doctrines, a deep-seated principle in our human nature, — a law of life, which we Protestants have had the folly to repudiate. We admire and reverence the beautiful old cathedrals which our Roman Catholic ancestors built and endowed. If we have not inherited them, we have, at least, appropriated them and made them ours; we worship God in them, we say our prayers in them after our own hearts. Can we not also appropriate and turn to account some of the institutions they have left us, — inform them with a spirit more consonant with our national character and the requirements of the age, and dedicate them anew to good and holy purposes ? What prevents us from using Sisters of Charity, as well as fine old cathedrals and colleges, for pious ends, and as a means of social benefit? Are we as stern, as narrow-minded, as deficient in real, loving faith as were our puritanical forefathers, when they not only defaced and desecrated, but would

gladly, if they could, have levelled to the earth
and utterly annihilated those monuments of
human genius and human devotion? Luckily
they stand in their beauty, to elevate the minds
and hearts of us, the descendants of those
who built and dedicated them, and who boast
that we have reformed, not destroyed the
Church of Christ!— and let me say that these
institutions of female charity, to which I have
referred, — institutions which had their source
in the deep heart of humanity, and in the
teaching of a religion of love, — let me say
that these are better and more beautiful and
more durable than edifices of stone reared by
men's hands, and worthy to be preserved and
turned to pious uses, though we can well dis-
pense with some of those ornaments and ap-
pendages which speak to us no more.

It would take far too much time were I
to go over the history of the early ages of
Christendom, and show you that women, associated under the ruling civil and ecclesiastical powers, were then officially, but voluntarily,
employed in works of social good. That these

women should have been early associated with
the church, and held their duties by ecclesiastical appointment, was natural and necessary,
because all moral sway, and all moral influence, and all education, and every peaceful
and elevating pursuit, belonged, for many centuries, to the ecclesiastical order only. The
singular and beneficent power exercised by
the religious and charitable women in these
times is remarked by all writers, though none
of them refer it to a natural law, — a great
first cause. The whole of the early history of
Christianity is full of examples. I will give
you one which, on looking over these authorities, struck me vividly.

Paula, a noble Roman lady, a lineal de-
scendant of the Scipios and the Gracchi, is
mentioned among the first Christian women
remarkable for their active benevolence. In
the year 385 she quitted Rome, then still a
Pagan city; with the remains of a large fortune, which had been expended in aiding and
instructing a wretched and demoralized people, and, accompanied by her daughter, she

sailed for Palestine, and took up her residence in Bethlehem of Judea. There, as the story relates, she assembled round her a community of women " as well of noble estate as of middle and low lineage." They took no vows, they made no profession, but spent their days in prayer and good works, having especially a well-ordered hospital for the sick.

In the old English translation of her life there is a picture of this charitable lady which I cannot refrain from quoting : " She was marvellous debonair, and piteous to them that were sick, and comforted them, and served them right humbly ; and gave them largely to eat such as they asked ; but to herself she was hard in her sickness and scarce, for she refused to eat flesh how well she gave it to others, and also to drink wine. She was oft by them that were sick, and she laid the pillows aright and in point ; and she rubbed their feet, and boiled water to wash them ; and it seemed to her that the less she did to the sick in service, so much the less service did she to God, and deserved the less mercy ; therefore she was to them piteous and nothing to herself."

This picture, drawn fifteen hundred years ago, so quaintly graphic, and yet so touching in its simplicity, will, perhaps, bring before the mind's eye of those who listen to me, scenes of the same kind, scenes now enacting in the far, far East, where female ministry has been called upon to do like offices of mercy; — to wash the wounds and smooth the couch, and "lay the pillow aright," of the maimed, the war-broken, the plague-stricken soldier. But we must for awhile turn back to the past.

It is in the seventh century that we find these commuities of charitable women first mentioned under a particular appellation. We read in history that when Landry, Bishop of Paris, about the year 650, founded a hospital, since known as the Hotel Dieu, as a general refuge for disease and misery, he placed it under the direction of the *Hospitalières*, or nursing-sisters of that time, — women whose services are understood to have been voluntary, and undertaken from motives of piety. Innocent IV., who would not allow of any outlying religious societies, collected and united these hospital-sisters under the rule of the Augustine Order, making them amenable to the government and discipline of the Church. The novitiate or training of a *Sœur Hospitalière* was of twelve years' duration, after which she was allowed to make her profession. At that time, and even earlier, we find many hospitals expressly founded for the reception of the sick pilgrims and wounded soldiers returning from the East, and bringing with them strange and hitherto unknown forms of disease and suffering. Some of the largest hospitals in France and the Netherlands originated in this purpose, and were all served by the Hospitalières; and to this day the Hotel Dieu, with its one thousand beds, the hospital of St. Louis, with its seven hundred beds, and that of *La Pitié*, with its six hundred beds, are served by the same sisterhood, under whose care they were originally placed centuries ago.

For about five hundred years the institution of the *Dames*, or *Sœurs Hospitalières*, remained the only one of its kind. During this period it had greatly increased its numbers, and extended all through western Christendom; still it did not suffice for the wants of the age; and the thirteenth century, fruitful in all those results which a combination of wide-spread suffering and religious ferment naturally produces, saw the rise of another community of compassionate women destined to exercise a far wider influence. These were the *Sœurs Grises*, or Grey Sisters, so called at first, from the original color of their dress. Their origin was this: — the Franciscans (and other regular orders) admitted into their community a third or secular class, who did not seclude themselves in cloisters, who took no vows of celibacy, but were simply bound to submit to certain rules and regulations, and united together in works of charity, devoting themselves to visiting the sick in the hospitals or at their own homes, and doing good whereever and whenever called upon. Women of all classes were enrolled in this sisterhood. Queens, princesses, ladies of rank, wives of burghers, as well as poor widows and maidens. The higher class and the married women

occasionally served; the widows and unmarried devoted themselves almost entirely to the
duties of nursing the sick in the hospitals.
Gradually it became a vocation apart, and
a novitiate or training of from one to three
years was required to fit them for their profession.

The origin of the Béguines, so well known
in Flanders, is uncertain; but they seem to
have existed as hospital-sisters in the seventh
century, and to have been settled in communities at Liege and elsewhere in 1173. They
wear a particular dress, (the black gown, and
white hood,) but take no vows, and may leave
the community at any time, — a thing which
rarely happens.

No one who has travelled in Flanders, visited Ghent, Bruges, Brussels, or indeed any of
the Netherlandish towns, will forget the singular appearance of these, sometimes young
and handsome, but always staid, respectable-
looking women, walking about protected by
the universal reverence of the people, and
busied in their compassionate vocation. In

their few moments of leisure the Béguines are allowed to make lace and cultivate flowers, and they act under a strict self-constituted government, maintained by strict traditional forms. All the hospitals in Flanders are served by these Béguines. They have besides, attached to their houses, hospitals of their own, with a medical staff of physicians and surgeons, under whose direction, in all cases of difficulty, the sisters administer relief; and of the humility, skill, and tenderness with which they do administer it, I have never heard but one opinion;* nor did I ever meet with any one who had travelled in those

* Howard mentions them with due praise, as serving in their hospital at Bruges. "There are twenty of them ; they look very healthy; they rise at four, and are constantly employed about their numerous patients." "They prepare as well as administer the medicines. The Directress of the Pharmacy last year celebrated her jubilee or fiftieth year of her residence in the hospital." (P. 149.)

A recent traveller mentions their hospital of St. John at Bruges as one of the best conducted he had ever met with. "Its attendants, in their religious costume and with their nuns' head-dresses, moving about with a quiet tenderness and solicitude, worthy their name as 'Sisters of Charity;' and the lofty wards, with the white linen of the beds, present in every particular an example of the most accurate neatness and cleanliness.

countries who did not wish that some system
of the kind could be transferred to England.

In the fifteenth century (about 1443), when
Flanders was under the dominion of the
Dukes of Burgundy, a few of the Béguines
were summoned from Bruges to Beaune to
take charge of the great hospital founded
there by Rollin, the Chancellor of Philip the
Good. They were soon joined by others from
the neighboring districts, and this community
of nurses obtained the name of *Sœurs de Ste·
Marthe*, Sisters of St. Martha. It is worth
notice that Martha, who is represented in
Scripture as troubled about household cares
while her sister Mary " sat at the feet of Jesus,
and heard his words," was early chosen as the
patroness of those who, instead of devoting
themselves to a cloistered life of prayer and
contemplation, were bound by a religious
obligation to active secular duties. The hospital of Beaune, one of the most extensive
and best managed in France, is still served by
these sisters. Many hospitals in the South of
France, and three at Paris, are served by the
same community.

In Germany, the Sisters of Charity are styled "Sisters of St. Elizabeth," in honor of that benevolent enthusiast, Elizabeth of Hungary, whose pathetic story and beautiful legend have been rendered familiar to us by Mr. Kingsley's drama. When Joseph II. suppressed the nunneries throughout Austria and Flanders, the Elizabethan Sisters, as well as the Béguines, were excepted by an especial decree, "because of the usefulness of their vocation." At Vienna, a few years ago, I had the opportunity, through the kindness of a distinguished physician, of visiting one of the houses of these Elizabethan Sisters. There was an hospital attached to it of fifty beds, which had received about four hundred and fifty patients during the year. Nothing could exceed the propriety, order, and cleanliness of the whole establishment. On the ground-floor was an extensive "Pharmacie," a sort of Apothecaries' Hall; part of this was divided off by a long table or counter, and surrounded by shelves filled with drugs, much like an apothecary's shop; behind the counter two Sisters, with their sleeves tucked up, were

busy weighing and compounding medicines,
with such a delicacy, neatness, and exactitude
as women use in these matters.   On the outside of this counter, seated on benches or
standing, were a number of sick and infirm,
pale, dirty, ragged patients; and among them
moved two other Sisters, speaking to each in-
dividually in a low gentle voice, and with a
quiet authority of manner, that in itself had
something tranquillizing.   A physician and
surgeon, appointed by the Government, visited
this hospital, and were resorted to in cases of
difficulty, or where operations were necessary.
Here was another instance in which men and
women worked together harmoniously and
efficiently.   Howard, in describing the principal hospital at Lyons, which he praises for its
excellent and kindly management, as being
" so clean and so quiet," tells us that at that
time (1776), he found it attended by nine physicians and surgeons, and managed by twelve
Sisters of Charity.   " There were Sisters who
made up, as well as administered, all the medicines prescribed; for which purpose there was
a laboratory and apothecary's shop, the neatest

and most elegantly fitted up that can be conceived." *

I must notice, with due respect and admiration, another female community, also especially excepted by an Imperial decree when other religious orders were suppressed, and for the same reason; — the Ursulines. We may smile at the childish and melancholy legend of St. Ursula and her eleven thousand virgins, and at the skulls heaped up in a certain mouldy tawdry chapel at Cologne; but of the Ursulines, as a community, we may be allowed to think seriously and even reverently. Their peculiar vocation was the care and instruction of poor children. They had their infant and ragged schools long before we had thought of them. Even from time immemorial there had existed, as we have seen, numerous communities of women to nurse and to pray; and there were isolated instances of

---

* Howard also mentions the hospitals belonging to the order of Charity, in all countries, as the best regulated, the cleanest, the most tenderly served and managed of all he had met with. He mentions the introduction of iron bedsteads into one of their hospitals as something new to him. (In 1776.)

women in the higher ranks extraordinarily pious and learned; but a community espe-cially to take charge of children, to teach, to educate, and prepare and train teachers, was not known in Christendom till the institution of the Ursuline Sisters in 1537: this originated in Brescia. Angela da Brescia, a woman of birth and fortune, lost at an early age and in a painful manner, a young sister, to whom she was tenderly attached. At first her sorrow took refuge in prayer, seclusion, and pilgri-mages, after the fashion of that time. It then took another form, and for the sake of the lost sister she devoted herself to the charitable work of collecting and educating poor female children.

It is touching, it is sadly significant, to see how often the beneficent tendencies of women have, when acted out, taken their especial form from some deep domestic sorrow, or some strong bias of the affections. I could men-tion several examples I have known, where love or grief has thus modified the element of charity.

The institution of Angela da Brescia was

the first of its kind; and so unheard of at this time was the attempt of women to organize a systematic education for their own sex, that when Françoise de Saintonge undertook to found such an establishment at Dijon, she was hooted in the streets, and her father called together four doctors learned in the law, "*pour s'assurer qu'instruire des femmes n'était pas un œuvre du démon.*" Even after he had given his consent, he was afraid to countenance his daughter; and Françoise, unprotected, unaided, began her first community of Ursulines in a garret with five poor children. Twelve years afterwards she was almost carried in triumph through the streets of Dijon, bells ringing, flowers strewed in her path. She had succeeded, and the Church took her under its wing; and with that far-sighted wisdom which Mr. Macaulay has pointed out as so characteristic, at once appropriated her and her good works.

These educational institutions multiplied during the next two hundred years, that is, down to the middle of the last century. The

Ursuline Sisters behaved admirably during
the French Revolution, and though dispersed
and their houses suppressed, they followed
their vocation, and by collecting and teaching
the poor orphans of massacred parents, and
assisting the village Curés, they prevented a
mass of evil. As soon as order was restored
they were reinstated, but their establishments
have not since increased in number. The ex-
tension of secular schools in France and Germany, and the popularity of the Sisters of
Mercy, who unite the educational duties of
the Ursulines with those of the Hospitalières,
have in some degree superseded them. I
have, however, visited several of the Ursuline
houses; and I remember one in particular
which I visited five-and-twenty years ago.
To reach the school, where more than three
hundred children were assembled, I had to
pass through a room in which about sixty infants were lying in cradles or on mattresses,
while two of the Sisterhood were going about
with pap, and stilling as well as they could the
incessant whimpering and squealing; — it was
an absurd and yet a pathetic scene. These

were babies left by poor women who had gone
to their daily work, and were to return for
them in the afternoon; and this plan has since
been imitated in the admirable charity of
" *Les Crêches*" instituted at Paris, and similar
charities in this country.

Now I do not say that the education given
by those good Sisters was the best possible, —
far from it. It did not go much beyond the
a, b, c, the Catechism, and a little needle-
work, but it was not worse than that which
many of our dame schools afforded fifty years
ago ; and it established as a principle that
women might be permitted to teach as well
as to learn ; — a principle so familiar to us in
these days, that we quite forget to look back
to a period when it was a strange, unheard-of
novelty, and had to do battle against prejudices, both of the clergy and the people.

It can easily be imagined that institutions
like these, composed of such various ingredi-
ents, spread over such various countries and
over several centuries of time, should have
been subject to the influences of time ; though

from a deep-seated principle of vitality and necessity they seem to have escaped its vicissitudes, for they did not change in character or purpose, far less perish. That in ages of superstition they should have been superstitious, that in ages of ignorance they should have been ignorant, — debased in evil selfish times, by some alloy of selfishness and cupidity, — in all this there is nothing to surprise us; but one thing does seem remarkable. While the men who professed the healing art were generally astrologers and alchymists, dealing in charms and nativities, — lost in dreams of the Elixir Vitæ and the Philosopher's Stone, and in such mummeries and quackeries as made them favorite subjects for comedy and satire, — these simple Sisters, in their hospitals, were accumulating a vast fund of practical and traditional knowledge in the treatment of disease, and the uses of various remedies ; — knowledge which was turned to account and condensed into rational theory and sound method, when in the sixteenth century Surgery and Medicine first rose to the rank of experimental sciences, and were studied as such. The poor Hospitalières knew nothing of Galen and Hippocrates, but they could observe if they could not describe, and prescribe, if they could not demonstrate. Still, in the course of time great abuses had certainly crept into these religious societies, — not so bad or so flagrant, perhaps, as those which disgraced within a recent period many of our own incorporated charities, — but bad enough, and vitiating, if not destroying, their power to do good. The funds were sometimes misappropriated, the novices ill-trained for their work, the superiors careless, the Sisters mutinous, the treatment of the sick remained rude and empirical. Women of sense and feeling, who wished to enrol themselves in these communities, were shocked and discouraged by such a state of things. A reform became absolutely necessary.

This was brought about, and very effectually, about the middle of the seventeenth century.

Louise de Marillac, — better known as Madame Legras, when left a widow in the prime of life, could find, like Angela da Brescia, no

better refuge from sorrow than in active duties, undertaken " for the love of God." She
desired to join the Hospitalières, and was met
at the outset by difficulties, and even horrors,
which would have extinguished a less ardent
vocation, a less determined will. She set herself to remedy the evils, instead of shrinking
from them. She was assisted and encouraged
in her good work by a man endued with great
ability and piety, enthusiasm equal, and moral
influence even superior, to her own. This
was the famous Vincent de Paul, who had
been occupied for years with a scheme to reform thoroughly the prisons and the hospitals
of France. In Madame Legras he found a
most efficient coadjutor. With her charitable
impulses and religious enthusiasm, she united
qualities not always, not often, found in union
with them : a calm and patient temperament,
and that administrative faculty, indispensable
in those who are called to such privileged
work. She was particularly distinguished by
a power of selecting and preparing the instruments, and combining the means, through
which she was to carry out her admirable pur-

pose. With Vincent de Paul and Madame Legras was associated another person, Madame Goussaut, who besieged the Archbishop of Paris till what was refused to reason was granted to importunity, and they were permitted to introduce various improvements into the administration of the hospitals. Vincent de Paul and Louise Legras succeeded at last in constituting, not on a new, but on a renovated basis, the order of Hospitalières, since known as the Sisterhood of Charity. A lower class of Sisters were trained to act under the direction of the more intelligent and educated women. Within twenty years this new community had two hundred houses and hospitals; in a few years more it had spread over all Europe. Madame Legras died in 1660. Already before her death the women prepared and trained under her instructions, and under the direction of Vincent de Paul (and here we have another instance of the successful communion of labor), had proved their efficiency on some extraordinary occasions. In the campaigns of 1652 and 1658 they were sent to the field of battle, in groups of two and four

together, to assist the wounded. They were
invited into the besieged towns to take charge
of the military hospitals. They were particularly conspicuous at the siege of Dunkirk, and
in the military hospitals established by Anne
of Austria at Fontainebleau. When the plague
broke out in Poland in 1672, they were sent to
direct the hospitals at Warsaw, and to take
charge of the orphans, and were thus introduced into Eastern Europe; and, stranger
than all! they were even sent to the prison-
infirmaries where the branded *forçats* and condemned felons lay cursing and writhing in
their fetters. This was a mission for Sisters
of Charity which may startle the refined, or
confined, notions of Englishwomen in the
nineteenth century. It is not, I believe, generally known in this country that the same
experiment has been lately tried, and with
success, in the prisons of Piedmont, where the
Sisters were first employed to nurse the
wretched criminals perishing with disease and
despair; afterwards, and during convalescence,
to read to them, to teach them to read and to
knit, and in some cases to sing. The hardest

of these wretches had probably some remembrance of a mother's voice and look thus recalled, or he could at least feel gratitude for sympathy from a purer, higher nature. As an element of reformation, I might almost say of regeneration, this use of the feminine influence has been found efficient where all other means had failed.

Howard, — well named the Good, — when inquiring into the state of prisons, about the middle of the last century, found many of those in France, bad as they generally were, far superior to those in our own country; and he attributes it to the employment and intervention of women "in a manner," he says, "which had no parallel in England." In Paris, he tells us, there were religious women "authorized to take care that the sick prisoners were properly attended to; and who furnished the felons in the dungeons with clean linen and medicine, and performed kind offices to the prisoners in general." "The provincial jails, also, have charitable patronesses, who take care that the prisoners be not defrauded of their allowance, and procure them farther relief." This, you will observe, was at a period when in England felons, debtors, and untried prisoners were dying by inches of filth and disease and despair. No doubt we have much improved since then, but not so much as we ought to have done.

A living writer observes that "it is astonishing and mortifying to consider how little progress the British legislature has made beyond adopting tardily, partially, and in a vacillating spirit, the improvements suggested seventy-nine years ago by Howard." * The striking remarks and suggestions in respect to the influence of women in some of the hospitals and prisons abroad, which abound in Howard's works, do not seem to have been noticed or taken into account at all, — not even by the author of the excellent treatise from which I quote.

It appears to be substantiated by the united testimony of some of the greatest medical authorities among us, — by such men as Brodie, Clark, Holland, Owen, Forbes, Conolly,

* Combe "*On the Principles of Criminal Legislation,*" &c.

and Carpenter,—prefixed to the above-named
treatise, that "criminal legislation and prison
discipline will never attain to a scientific, con-
sistent, practical, and efficient character, until
they have become based on physiology of the
brain and nervous system;" or, as it is else-
whree expressed, "while the influence of organism on the dispositions and capacities of
men continues to be ignored." Then have
we not to consider, as the next step, *what* is to
influence the organism? Have we not to
consider whether there may not exist organic
influences arising out of contrasted yet harmo-
nious organisms,—mutual influences which
God has contemplated in those sacred and
universal relations which bind his creation
together, and which we ought reverently to
use for good, instead of allowing pernicious
quacks and sensualists most irreligiously to
misuse and abuse for evil?

It is difficult to believe in "invincible per-
tinacity in evil." Nevertheless, it does seem
that there are some few miserable creatures
who are, in respect to the moral organization,
what idiots are in respect to intellect. We

know, however, that a large proportion of the convicts in our prisons, and the sick in our hospitals, and the outcasts in our workhouses, are unhappy beings, who have never been brought into contact with goodness elevated by the religious principle, softened by the spirit of love, and refined by habitual gentleness and modesty; and we seem in these matters to be in such constant fear of doing mischief, that we have no courage to do good. We stand in such a dastardly terror of the ridicule which follows mistake or failure, that we ought to die of inward shame, while thus entrenching ourselves in the negative good, instead of bravely meeting the positive evil. The hardest thing which visitors of prisons have to contend with in the wretched delinquents, is not so much the propensity to evil as the ignorance of, and disbelief in, goodness; on men of this stamp and on young offenders, judicious female influence would probably have effect where men in authority, though not less well intentioned and equally judicious, arouse only feelings of suspicion, sullenness, and resistance.

From recent inquiries I learn that the system of employing Sisters of Charity as visitors in the prisons of Piedmont continues to work well, and that none of the evils which might have been apprehended have in any instance occurred.* But supposing they *had* occurred; a hundred mistakes and failures at the outset could not invalidate the principle that what had once succeeded on a large scale would, under similar conditions, again succeed : that the expedient of bringing the female mind and temperament to bear on the masculine brain, (and of course *vice versâ*,) as a physical and moral resource, might be worth a thought, being in accordance with that law of nature or Divine ordinance which placed the two sexes under mutual and sympathetic influences; not always, as the stupid and profligate suppose, for evil and temptation, but for good and for healing: not in one or two relations of life, but in every possible relation

* While these sheets are going through the press, I learn that by a recent decree of the Piedmontese Chamber of Deputies all the conventual religious orders and monasteries in Piedmont are to be suppressed, but from this decree the active Sisterhoods of Charity are excepted.

in which they can be approximated. This suggestion I merely throw out here as not unworthy of the consideration of our physicians, moralists, and legislators. I leave it to them and to time, and I proceed.

At the commencement of the French Revolution the Sisterhood of Charity had four hundred and twenty-six houses in France, and many more in other countries; the whole number of women then actively employed was about six thousand. During the Reign of Terror, the Superior (Mdlle. Duleau), who had become a Sister of Charity at the age of nineteen, and was now sixty, endeavored to keep the society together, although suppressed by the Government; and in the midst of the horrors of that time, — when so many nuns and ecclesiastics perished miserably, — it appears that the feeling of the people protected these women, and I do not learn that any of them suffered public or personal outrage. As soon as the Consular government was established, the indispensable Sisterhood was recalled by a decree of the Minister of the Interior.

I cannot resist giving you a few passages from the preamble to this edict, — certainly very striking and significant, — as I find it quoted in a little book on " Hospitals and Sisterhoods" now before me.

It begins thus: —

" Seeing that the services rendered to the sick can only be properly administered by those whose vocation it is, and who do it in the spirit of love; —

" Seeing, farther, that among the hospitals of the Republic those are in all ways best served wherein the female attendants have adhered to the noble example of their predecessors, whose only object was to practise a boundless love and charity; —

" Seeing that the members still existing of this society are now growing old, so that there is reason to fear that an order which is a glory to the country may shortly become extinct; —

" It is decreed that the Citoyenne Duleau, formerly Superior of the Sisters of Charity, is authorized to educate girls for the care of the hospitals," &c.

I confess I should like to see an act of our

parliament beginning with such a preamble!
I confess I should like to see an act of our
parliament beginning with a recognition that
women do exist as a part of the community,
whose responsibilities are to be acknowledged,
and whose capabilities are to be made available, not separately, but conjointly with those
of men. For that surely must be a defective
legislation which takes for granted only the
crimes, the vices, the mistakes of humanity,
and makes no account of its virtues, its affections, and its capabilities.

Previous to the Revolution, the chief military hospitals and the naval hospitals at Brest,
Saint-Malo, and Cherbourg, had been placed
under the management of the Sisters of Charity. During the Reign of Terror, those Sisters
who refused to quit their habit and religious
bond were expelled; but as soon as order was
restored, they were recalled by the naval and
military authorities, and returned to their
respective hospitals, where their reappearance
was hailed with rejoicing, and even with tears.
At present the naval hospitals at Toulon and

Marseilles, in addition to those I have mentioned, are served by these women, acting *with*, as well as *under*, authority.

The whole number of women included in these charitable orders was, in the year 1848, at least, twelve thousand. They seem to have a quite marvellous ubiquity. I have myself met with them not only at Paris, Vienna, Milan, Turin, Genoa, but at Montreal, Quebec, and Detroit; on the confines of civilization; in Ireland, where cholera and famine were raging. Everywhere, from the uniform dress and a certain similarity in the placid expression and quiet deportment, looking so like each other, that they seemed, whenever I met them, to be but a multiplication of one and the same person. In all the well-trained Sisters of Charity I have known, whether Protestant or Roman Catholic, I have found a mingled bravery and tenderness, if not by nature, by habit; and a certain tranquil self-complacency, arising, not from self-applause, but out of that very abnegation of self which had been adopted as the rule of life.*

---

* " A letter from the Piræus, dated the 27th of November, says, — ' The cholera is at this moment raging at Athens with

I have now given you a rapid and most imperfect sketch of what has been done by an
organized system of charity in the Roman
Catholic Church.

I am no friend to nunneries. I do not like
even the idea of Protestant nunneries, which I
have heard discussed and warmly advocated.
I conceive that any large number of women
shut up together in one locality, with no occupation connecting them actively and benevo-
lently with the world of humanity outside,
with all their interests centred within their
walls, would not mend each other, and that
such an atmosphere could not be perfectly
healthy, spiritually, morally, or physically.
There would necessarily ensue, in lighter characters, frivolity, idleness, and sick disordered
fancies; and in superior minds, ascetic pride,
gloom, and impatience. But it is very different with the active orders, and I should cer-

great violence. The inhabitants, who had begun to return to
the capital, are again flying in all directions. The Sisters of
Charity have spontaneously offered to take care of the sick,
and the religious prejudices of the country have yielded
before the admitted capacity of the Sisterhood in all that concerns the treatment of the sick, and before the gentle influence which they exercise wheresoever they pass.' " (Times,
Dec. 15, 1854.)

tainly like to see amongst us some institutions
which, if not exactly like them, should supply
their place.

In speaking on the subject with intelligent
and experienced men and women, I have generally met with the strongest sympathy; but
sometimes also with the vague, sweeping objection, that such communities are quite con-
trary to the spirit of the Reformed Church,
and among Protestants quite impracticable.
The worse for us, if it were true; but is it
true?

The experiment *has* been tried, an attempt
has been made, to found such an institution in
a Protestant community, though not in this
country; it has not yet stood the test of centuries, but let us see what has been done within a period of thirty years.

At Kaiserswerth on the Rhine, a small town
near Dusseldorf, a manufactory had been established during the last war, in which the workmen employed were almost all Protestants.
In 1822 the manufacturer became bankrupt,

and the workmen were reduced to poverty.
Their pastor, Mr. Fliedner, then a very young
man, travelled through Holland and England
to collect from sympathizing friends the
necessary funds to support a church in his
small parish. In this, we are told, he fully
succeeded, and, it is added, "this was the
smallest part of the result of his journey."
While in England he became acquainted with
Mrs. Fry. It was the meeting of two most
congenial minds, and his attention was at
once turned to the objects which then occupied
her. On his return home he originated at
Dusseldorf the first society in Germany for the
improvement of prison discipline. Experience
in prisons pointed out to him some ways ot
doing good which came within his then small
means. He had been struck with compassion
for the desolate condition of women who,
when discharged from prison, already depraved by bad habits and without the means of
subsistence, "are in a manner *forced* back into
crime." With one female criminal, and one
voluntary assistant, he founded his penitentiary in a little summer-house in his garden.

This was in 1833. In the following year he met with a second volunteer assistant, and collected together nine more penitents, of whom eight had been more than once in prison. This part of the institution, memorable as the first beginning of an establishment, which has since extended to so many and various branches, has always been kept entirely separate from the rest. A general hospital, a lunatic asylum, an orphan asylum, an infant school, became so many seminaries for training hospital nurses, teachers (*i. e.* instructing Sisters), and visitors of the poor (called parish deaconesses). On these I do not dwell at present, for we must confine ourselves to the theme in hand. It is the hospital at Kaiserswerth which constitutes the most important part of the establishment, and is likely to be the most extensive and permanent in its effects.

In 1836 Mr. Fliedner established his hospital in the deserted manufactory. He had been led to think of it partly from the want of good nurses for the sick; partly from regret, as he said himself, to see " how much good female

power was wasted;" partly from a perception
that the women who had voluntarily come
forward to assist him required a larger sphere
for the exercise of their faculties. He began,
as usual, humbly enough, — with one patient
and one nurse. Within the first year the
number of voluntary nurses was seven, and
the number of patients received and nursed
was sixty, besides twenty-eight nursed at their
own houses. The hospital contained in 1854,
one hundred and twenty beds, which were
generally full, and more than six thousand
patients have been received since its commencement.

But the chief purpose of this hospital is to
serve as a training-school for nursing Sisters.
Every one who offers herself (and there is no
want of offers) is taken on trial for six months,
during which she must pay for her board, and
wears no distinctive dress. If she persists in
her vocation and is accepted, she undergoes a
further probation (like the novitiate of the
Roman Catholic Sisters) of from one to three
years. She then puts on the hospital dress,
and is boarded and lodged gratis. The male

wards are served by men-nurses, of whom
there are five, who have been educated in the
hospital, and are under the authority of the
Sisters. They sleep in the male wards, and sit
up in case of need. It is added, that " the
most fastidious could find nothing to object to
in the intercourse which takes place between
patients, surgeon, and Sisters."

As no inducement is offered to these Protestant Sisters any more than in the Catholic
Orders, no prospect of pecuniary reward, or
praise or reputation, nothing, in short, but the
opportunity of working for the sake of God
and humanity, so, if this does not appear sufficient for them, they are dismissed. After they
have been accepted and made their profession,
they receive yearly a small sum for clothing,
and nothing more; they can receive no fee or
reward from those they serve, but in age or
illness the parent institution is bound to receive and provide for them.

A certain number of these Sisters obtain a
particular education to fit them for parish
visitors. The absolute necessity that women
should be especially trained in order to make

good and efficient parish visitors is apparent; for it is wonderfully and often pathetically absurd to see with what a large stock of goodness and conscientious anxiety, and what a small stock of experience, knowledge, and sympathy with their objects, some excellent women set off on their task as lady visitors of the poor. A number of the Sisters, trained properly, have been sent to distant towns and villages, at the request of clergymen and visiting societies. Others are occupied in nursing in private families, their services being repaid to the parent institution. The excellent Mr. Fliedner and his wife still conduct it, and receive their best reward, had they sought any, in the success of their undertaking. There are at present on the establishment one hundred and ninety Sisters, of whom sixty-two are still probationers or learners. Of the Hospital Sisters, eighty are stationed in different hospitals in Germany; five in London; three at Constantinople (they are probably by this time at Scutari); five at Jerusalem; two at Smyrna, and two at Pittsburg, in the United States; — making in all, ninety-seven women'

properly trained and educated, and fully employed in their beneficent vocation.

Let me add, for it is a matter of interest at
present, that Miss Florence Nightingale went
through a regular course of training at Kaiserswerth, before she took charge of the Female
Sanitarium in London.

In imitation of Mr. Fliedner's establishment,
a similar institution for the training of Protestant nurses and teachers has been opened at
Paris; another at Strasbourg; another at Berlin, under the especial protection of the Queen
of Prussia, and under the direction of the
Baroness Rantzau, who had previously gone
through a complete course of instruction and
experience at Kaiserswerth. The number of
nursing Sisters in the Berlin hospital is twenty-
eight, and there are twelve probationers. A
similar establishment was founded at Dresden
by the late excellent and amiable Countess
Alfred Hohenthal (*née* Princess Biron), in
which twenty-one women are under a course

of instruction. There are besides ten other institutions, which I find described as existing in different localities, but all emanating from the same origin, and containing altogether not less than four hundred and twenty-nine members. So that it seems no longer a question as to whether, in Protestant communities, a number of women *can* be properly trained and organized for purposes of social benefit, authorized and employed by the Government, aided and directed by intelligent and good men, and sustained by public opinion. I consider that the question has been answered; and I must repeat my strong conviction, that such a communion of labor and of love, as I have endeavored to describe, is not a thing of country, creed, or custom, but is founded in the very laws of our being; — in that self-same law which is the basis of domestic life; that it is one of the main conditions of social happiness and morals; and that the neglect of it in any country or community strikes at the heart of all that is best in men and women, increases the faults of both and their ignorance of each other, and tends consequently to the ultimate degradation and misery of all society.*

* For intelligible reasons I have made no reference in this lecture to what has been considered as the particular province of all Sisters of Charity deserving the name, — the management of Penitentiaries and Houses of Refuge for the erring and the fallen of their own sex. I shall merely observe, that there is no department of active benevolence requiring more careful preparation and more especial instruction than this. The treatment of women whose habitual existence has been a perpetual outrage of their nature, *must* be special and exceptional ; and I do not think that this is always well understood by the excellent and virtuous ladies who undertake to manage these scarcely manageable creatures. They are thought to be mentally and morally depraved, when in fact it is often the complete derangement of the nervous system, brought on by vice and disease, which produces those changeful moods, those fits of sullenness, excitability, obtuseness, insolence, and desperation by which I have seen the most benevolent filled with disgust and the most hopeful with despondency. I believe it to be true that women, even from the superior delicacy of the moral and physical organization, can be more thoroughly, hopelessly, and constitutionally vitiated than men ; this I have often heard urged as an argument for rejecting and punishing them when bad, never for protecting and sparing them when good. Such forms of malady in such sacrificed creatures are best treated in the country, by avoiding too much sedentary employment, by active exercise and really hard work in the open air, by talking to them and suffering them to talk as little as possible of themselves, and by gradually opening the mind to religious impressions without exciting resistance or despondency. No mere impulse of pity, no mere power of will, can enable any one to undertake this most difficult mission, which ought to combine the vocation of charity with some of the qualifications of a physician.

Let us now look at home, and consider what has been done in our own country. Is there any hope, any possibility, of organizing into some wise and recognized system the talent and energy, the piety and tenderness of our women for the good of the whole community.

The subject becomes one of awful importance when we consider, that in the last census of 1851, there appears an excess of the female over the male population of Great Britain of more than half-a-million, the proportion being one hundred and four women to every one hundred men. How shall we employ this superfluity of the "feminine element" in society, how turn it to good and useful purposes, instead of allowing it to run to waste? Take of these five hundred thousand superfluous women only the one-hundredth part, say five thousand women, who are willing to work for good, to join the communion of labor, under a directing power, if only they knew how, — if only they could *learn* how, — best to do their work, and if employment were open to them, — what a phalanx it would be if properly organized!

Everywhere I find the opinion of thoughtful and intelligent men corroborative of my own observations and conclusions. In spite of the adverse feeling of " *that other public,* to which *we,* the sensible reflecting public, are not in the least degree related," * — in spite of routine and prejudice, — the feeling of those who in the long run will lead opinion, is for us. They say: " In all our national institutions we want the help of women. In our hospitals, prisons, lunatic asylums, workhouses, reformatory schools, elementary schools, — everywhere we want efficient women, and none are to be found prepared or educated for our purpose." The men whom I have heard speak thus, seem to regard this infusion of a superior class of working women into our public institutions as a new want, a new expedient. They do not seem to feel or recognize the profound truth, that the want now so generally felt and acknowledged, arises out of a great unacknowledged law of the Creator, a law old as creation itself, which makes

* Vide " HOUSEHOLD WORDS," vol. xi. No. 254

the moral health of the community to depend on the co-operation of woman in all work that concerns the well-being of man. For as I have said before, it is not in one or two relations, but in all the possible relations of life, in which men and women are concerned, that they must work together for mutual improvement, and the general good; and I return to the principle laid down at first, " the communion of love and the communion of labor." *

* Since this lecture was delivered I find the following passage in a paper on " Municipal Government," published by the Manchester Statistical Society.

" In carrying out these and various other objects of importance, I am persuaded that the agency of the female sex is necessary, and that without the well organized aid of benevolent and educated women, municipal government will ever remain limited and imperfect. I do not contemplate the formal election of females to municipal offices, although this would appear from ' Grant on Corporations,' not to be without precedent in England, where women, we know, are still, by Law, eligible as overseers of the poor, and capable of filling the highest office in the kingdom."

" A number of years ago, in a paper read before this Society, entitled ' Thoughts on the Excess of Adult Females in the Population of Great Britain, with reference to its Causes and Consequences,' I endeavored to show that the female sex, in Christian countries, are probably designed for duties more in number and in importance than have yet been assigned them. The reasons were, that above the twentieth

" In England," (it has been truly said,) " there are no men to be found systematically trained to the moral management of convicts, such as are to be found in Germany and other

year, in all fully-peopled states, whether in Europe or in North America, women considerably outnumber the other sex ; and that, as this excess is produced by causes which remain in steady operation, we detect therein a natural law, and may allowably infer that it exists for beneficent social ends, — ends, amongst others, such as those I am attempting to explain and recommend.

" I own that I cannot but regard the population of our large towns as in a very unsatisfactory state ; and feel persuaded that the wisest, — the best devised, — regulations *enforced by the police alone,* as is the case at present, will not succeed ; but I think that a body of educated ladies for each ward, *acting in concert with the legal authorities,*" (*that is to say, men and women working together,*) " would be found of wonderful service in detecting radical evils, especially the sources of preventible poverty; or what is much the same, the various temptations which beset the laborer's family, from bad laws and defective arrangements of different kinds, owing to which the amount of sickness, poverty, immorality, and unhappiness is at all times appallingly great."—(*Suggestions for the Improvement of Municipal Government in populous Manufacturing Towns,* by John Roberton, published in the Transactions of the Manchester Statistical Society. 1854.)

I do not venture to give any opinion with regard to the " Suggestions " here thrown out in reference to women, — for I have never thought about Municipal Government or the duties of Overseers, — but I extract the above passages as showing the ideas entertained and openly expressed by some experienced and intelligent men.

countries. It is the bane of the English system of government throughout, that it does not render the public service, in its various civil departments, a series of professions, for which men must be specially educated and trained; and the great English universities, in consequence, do not educate young men for any pursuits on earth, except those of a gentleman and a scholar."* In the same manner the education given to our women is merely calculated to render them ornamental and well-informed; but it does not train them, even those who are so inclined and fitted by nature, to be effective instruments of social improvement. Whether men, without the assistance and sympathetic approval of well-educated women, are likely to improve and elevate the moral tone of society, or work out good in any especial sphere or profession, is, I think, hardly a question. God, who created the human race male and female, did not make human culture and progress to depend on one half of it.

* Combe "*On the Principles of Criminal Legislation and the Practice of Prison Discipline.*"

I believe the employment of well trained women in the reformatory schools for juvenile delinquents, which are to be established under a late Act of Parliament, has been already suggested. It is a great advance in opinion that the possible good of such a measure should be spoken of in high quarters. For about ten years, perhaps, the means of carrying it out may be considered and debated; in another ten years, some plan will be proposed; and in another ten years, perhaps, adopted; for such is the usual progress of any great moral movement in "that other public," — that self-satisfied, unreasoning, cowardly, somnolent public which *we* repudiate; wherein such topics are discussed with reference merely to custom and expediency, not to justice and necessity, — with reference to human laws, which can be made and unmade, not with reference to divine laws, immutable principles of life, which cannot be violated or neglected in any social community, without bringing in the elements of demoralization and decay.

And respecting that movement in favor of

the wretched children who so long infested
our streets and crammed our gaols, and for
whom a long delayed measure of wisdom and
justice was obtained last year, may I not be
permitted to say how much that cause owed
to the unceasing exertions of three admirable
women, true Sisters of Charity, who, to my
knowledge, have been occupied in this good
work for twenty years? With regard to the
first of these ladies, her attention was early
called to the subject, and she never ceased to
advocate, and, I may say, to agitate the theme.
She moved in high society; she was nobly
born and connected, eloquent, and clever, and
lively; and she made use of all these advantages to promote the settled purpose of her
mind. She failed in some attempts to execute
plans of reform without the legislative sanction, but she was not discouraged. She attacked Home Secretaries, and she plagued
magistrates; no M. P. was safe from her, no
Minister of State. Like the woman in Scripture who persecuted the unjust judge, she
made herself listened to by her " much speaking," and at length *leavened* the society in

which she moved with her own feelings, her own hopes, her own faith. The second lady I refer to was one who carried out into action, and tested by practical experience, and illustrated by published documents, by well-digested facts, and eloquent reasoning, the truths which her sister in beneficence had advocated. Need I name Mary Carpenter, — a name publicly and inseparably connected with the cause? When called up before a Committee of the House of Commons, her evidence was so clear, so conclusive, and given with such self-possession and precision, as well as feminine feeling, that I have heard those who were present express their admiration, — their conviction that the testimony and the arguments of this excellent woman had, in fact, turned the scale. The third lady I will not name. She not only brought to the question a noble and powerful intellect, but she invested in it a portion of her affections, — a part of her very heart; she gave it all the advantages of her character and position; and she had wealth which enabled her to purchase and pay well for the exertions of others, their brains, their pens. When, last year, after more than twenty years had thus passed, the Act of Parliament was obtained, (which, however inadequate in some respects, did at least recognize the principle for which they were contending,) was there not joy in those three hearts? I know there was. I had no right to share in the triumph; I had done nothing; but I could sympathize, — as you do! God forbid that I should seek to lessen the value of the voluntary aid, the indefatigable exertions, the eloquent pleading of those wise and good men who were united in this cause, and at length succeeded in gaining it; but let me say that this was a strong instance of what I mean by the "communion of love and the communion of labor," carried out into social public objects.

It is perfectly notorious that in the reformatory and elementary schools for boys in America, great use is made of female influence and tuition. Women were first resorted to from a scarcity of masters, and the greater cheapness of female labor. What was at first a matter of expediency and necessity, has since become matter of choice, for the experiment has been crowned with success, and has been productive of far more good than was at first contemplated; and I believe that in the Schools or Houses of Detention contemplated here under the new Act of Parliament for young delinquents, the teaching and influence of well-trained gentlewomen invested with an official authority, might exercise incalculable good. " I can manage any number of naughty boys," said a lady who is celebrated among us as a Protestant Sister of Charity on a large scale, " no matter how wicked and mutinous. I *feel* that I have the power to subdue them; but I confess I have great difficulty with girls, — I do not know why." The cause, if we looked to Nature and her wise adaptations, would not be far to seek.*

---

* I have heard of a lady now (or very lately) residing near Harvard University, " who, amid the duties and cares of her own household, fitted many young men for those colleges which neither she nor any of her sex were, as students, ever allowed to enter. For twenty years this lady has been accustomed to receive under her roof those students of the Univer-

With regard to the employment of women in the lunatic asylums, I can only say that I have the testimony of men of large experience that feminine aid, influence, presence, would in many cases be most beneficial in the male wards.* Of course there are certain cases in which it would be dangerous, inadmissible;

sity who were rusticated for various offences; and, while kneading her bread or plying her needle, she assisted them in their classical studies, and mended their manners at the same time."

It is well known that one of the best and most popular teachers of navigation and nautical mathematics and astronomy in England is a lady — Mrs. Janet Taylor; that her classes are celebrated, and numerously attended by men who have been at sea, as well as by youths preparing for the merchant service.

* Of the Salpêtrière, Howard says, that, at the time of his visit (1776), the whole house "was kept clean and quiet by the great attention of the religious women who served it; but it was terribly crowded, containing more than five thousand poor, sick, and insane persons."

He describes the Hospital "des Incurables" at Paris, containing four hundred aged and infirm persons, as admirably served and managed by forty Sisters.

Again: — "Here (at Ghent) is a foundation belonging to the Béguines for the reception of twelve men who are insane, and for sick and aged women. The insane have, when requisite, assistance from their own sex; and the tenderness with which both these and the poor women are treated by the Sisters, gave me no little pleasure."—(*Howard on Prisons,* p. 145.)

but it is their opinion that in most cases it
would have a soothing, sanitary, harmonizing
effect. In reference to this subject let me mention a lady with whom I have the honor to be
personally acquainted. She is a native of the
United States, and has given her attention for
many years to the management of the insane,
and the improvement of mad-houses. She
has travelled alone through every part of the
United States, — from New York to Chicago,
from New Orleans to Quebec. She has been
the means of founding nineteen new asylums,
and improving and enlarging a greater number. She has won those in power to listen to
her, and is considered in her own country a
first-rate authority on such subjects, just as
Mrs. Fry was here in regard to prisons, Mrs.
Chisholm in regard to emigration, and Miss
Carpenter in regard to juvenile criminals. As
to the use of trained women in lunatic asylums, I will say no more at present, but throw
it out as a suggestion to be dealt with by
physiologists, and entrusted to *time*.

With reference to the employment of wo-

men as a higher order of nurses in hospitals,
late events might almost render it superfluous
to speak at all, but that it is important to my
present theme to look back to the history of
public opinion on this subject.

I find that more than thirty years ago, —
long before the institution at Kaiserswerth existed or was thought of, — the late Dr. Gooch
entertained the idea of establishing in this
country some institution analogous to that
of the Sisters of Charity. Dr. Gooch is to
this day a great medical authority as a physician; he was also a philanthropist and a
philosopher. During a tour in Belgium he
had been struck — as all are struck — by the
institution of the Béguines, their well-ordered
hospitals, and their general efficiency in visiting and prescribing for the sick poor. He
corresponded with Southey on this subject,
and at the end of the second volume of
Southey's " Colloquies" may be found the
ideas he had brought from the Netherlands
and communicated to his friend: also two
letters published in the " Medical Gazette,"

and signed " A Country Surgeon," which are
now known to have been written by Dr.
Gooch. There is also a most eloquent exposition of Southey's own opinions, holding
up to us the example of the Béguines and the
Sisters of Charity ; and, which is curious, he
seems to have put his trust in Quakerism
rather than in our own Church, (the church
which he so devoutly admired and defended;)
and he even hoped that Mrs. Opie would do
for our hospitals what Mrs. Fry had done for
our prisons. But he mistook the character of
Mrs. Opie : it was *not* the vocation of that
amiable and gifted woman.

You must permit me to read one or two
passages from these letters written by Dr.
Gooch in 1825, because of their beauty, and
because of their good sense. He begins by
describing at length the appearance and manners of the Sisters of Charity in France and
Belgium ; their respectable, kindly appearance;
their peculiar yet appropriate dress ; the care,
the tenderness, the skill with which they attended on the sick. He then adds : —

" Let all real Christians join and found an order of women like the Sisters of Charity in Catholic countries : let them be selected for good plain sense, kindness of disposition, indefatigable industry, and deep piety ; let them receive, — not a technical and scientific, — but a practical medical education. For this purpose let them be placed both as nurses and pupils in the hospitals of Edinburgh and London, or in the county hospitals ; let their attention be pointed by the attending physicians to the particular symptoms by which he distinguishes the disease ; let them be made as familiar with the best remedies (which are always few) as they are with barley-water, gruel, and beef-tea ; let them learn the rules by which the remedies are to be employed ; let them be examined frequently on these subjects, in order to see that they carry these rules clearly in their heads ; let books be framed for them containing the essential rules of practice, —briefly, clearly, and untechnically written. Let such women, thus educated, be distributed among the country parishes of the kingdom, and be maintained by parish allowance, which now goes to the parish surgeon, who should be resorted to only in difficult cases; let them be examined every half year by competent physicians about the state of their medical knowledge. Let this be done, and I fearlessly predict that my friend, and all those who are similarly situated and zealous with himself, will no longer complain that their sick flock suffer from medical neglect.

"It may be objected that women with such an education would form a bad substitute for a scientific medical attendance. Be it remembered, however, that the choice is not between such women and a profound and perfect physician or surgeon (if there is such a person), but between such women and the ordinary run of country apothecaries; the latter laboring under the additional disadvantage of wanting time for the application of what skill they have."

"If any attempt should be made to introduce Sisters of Charity into England, I would

advise the experiment to be made at first on a
small scale.   They should be not mere nurses
and religious instructors, but a set of religious
female physicians.   I would select two or
three women, — not superannuated servants
in search of a quiet livelihood, who are thinking of nothing but how to make money with
the least trouble, and who would apply, or be
recommended, in crowds for such a purpose, —
but women originally and habitually of a
higher order, young enough to learn, yet old
enough to be sick of worldly vanities; in
short, with strong sense, a good education,
and something of the devotee (there are many
such).   I would place them in some hospital
under an experienced, clear-headed, practical
physician, who should explain to them in un-
technical language, as they went from bed to
bed, signs by which he is guided in the choice
of his remedies.   I would sharpen their attention and assist their memories by frequent
examinations into their knowledge; always
remembering that it is not safely deposited in
the mind until the student can state it and
apply it herself.

" This system of instruction should continue until my Sisters of Charity have acquired a readiness in detecting all ordinary diseases, in selecting the guiding symptoms, and in the use of that short list of remedies which even medical men find sufficient in pauper practice. When they are ripe for my purpose, I would (taking a hint from the Sœurs de Charité) station two of them in a cottage placed in the centre of some country district. I would have them maintained partly from the parish funds, partly by the voluntary subscriptions of the opulent people of the neighborhood, and partly by those of the charitable and religious world. Their kindness and care would soon ensure the good will of the poor. A few cures would be followed by medical reputation, and the cottagers of the district would soon have reason to bless the hour when these useful women settled in their neighborhood."

This plan may appear at first sight somewhat Utopian; but is it so really? Could there be a better way of employing some of our superfluous women?

I must quote one more passage : —

" Many will think that it is impossible to
impart a useful knowledge of medicine to women who are ignorant of anatomy, physiology,
and pathology. A profound knowledge, of
course, would not, but a very useful degree of
it might: — a degree which, combined with
kindness and assiduity, would be far superior
to that which the country poor receive at
present. I have known matrons and sisters
of hospitals with more practical tact in the
detection and treatment of disease than half
the young surgeons by whom the country
poor are commonly attended."

These were the words of an eminent practical physician thirty years ago. No result
followed, — scarcely was public attention
wakened to the subject; the writer went
down to his last rest with a favorite idea
unaccomplished; but heaven and earth shall
pass away before one particle of that truth
which has emanated from the benevolent,
trusting, faithful spirit shall fail and perish.

The feeling with which the expedition of the lady-nurses to the East was regarded by the lower order of medical men was exhibited in many ways not very creditable. It reminded me of what had taken place some ten or twelve years ago when the female School of Design was first projected; when a petition was drawn up and handed round for signature by a certain set of artists and engravers, praying that the women might not be taught at the expense of government " arts which would interfere with the employment of men, and take the bread out of their mouths." The men who signed and circulated this precious document were not wicked or bad-hearted. I dare say they meant well. They only took that selfish, one-sided view of the subject natural in persons who had been ill-educated, and were totally ignorant of the bearings of any large moral or social question. Of the obvious benefit such an institution might afford to their daughters or sisters, thus lightening the burthen on men with large families, they did not think ; — far less on the right of every human being to the due cultivation and exercise of every good gift "that cometh from above." Had their views been listened to, how many hundreds of young women who are now maintaining themselves or helping their families, would be perishing on the streets, in prisons, in work-houses! And who would have been the better? Of the artists who signed that petition some are dead, and some whom I know would not like to be reminded of their share in it, — are indeed thoroughly ashamed of it. I believe that if among medical men a petition were now handed round for signature, praying that women should not be taught at the expense of government, the physical and moral conditions of health, the symptoms of disease, the preparation of the best remedies and the rules for administering them, lest they should "interfere with the employments of men, and take the bread out of their mouths," — I am afraid there are well intentioned and well educated men who would at this time be induced to sign such a paper; but I believe that twenty — even ten — years hence, they would look back upon their signatures and the whole trans-

action with as much disgust and amazement
as is now excited by the exploded attempt to
crush and sneer down the female School at
Marlborough House.

As I have said, — no immediate result followed upon the suggestion of Dr. Gooch; but
the good thus sown only slept, like the seed
in wintry ground.

A few years ago, several intelligent and
benevolent persons, men and women, who
had had opportunities of studying the management of the institution at Kaiserswerth,
conceived the idea that a similar institution,
for similar purposes, might be founded in
England, and that both our government and
our clergy would be induced to co-operate in
such a plan, if once public interest could be
excited in its favor. It was admitted on all
sides, that the general management of our
hospitals and charitable institutions exhibited
the want of female aid, such as exists in the
hospitals abroad, — the want of a moral, religious, intelligent, sympathizing influence,

combined with the physical cares of a common nurse. Some inquiry was made into the general character of hospital nurses, and the qualifications desired; and what were these qualifications? Obedience, presence of mind, cheerfulness, sobriety, patience, forbearance, judgment, kindness of heart, a light delicate hand, a gentle voice, a quick eye; — these were the qualities enumerated as not merely desirable, but necessary, in a good and efficient nurse, — a long list of virtues not easily to be purchased for 14*l*. 10*s*. a year! — qualifications, indeed, which in their union would form an admirable woman in any class of life, and fit her for any sphere of duty, from the highest to the lowest. In general, however, the requirements of our medical men are much more limited; they consider themselves fortunate if they can ensure obedience and sobriety even, without education, tenderness, intelligence, religious feeling, or any high principle of duty. On the whole, the testimony brought before us is sickening. Drunkenness, profligacy, violence of temper, horribly coarse and brutal language, — these are com-

mon. We know that there are admirable exceptions, more particularly in the great London
Hospitals; and the spectacle of devoted charity exhibited by the officials in the Middlesex
Hospital during the late visitation of the
cholera must be fresh in the memory of those
whom I address. Still, the reverse of the picture is more generally true. The toil is great,
the duties disgusting, the pecuniary remuneration small in comparison; so that there is
nothing to invite the co-operation of a better
class of women, but the highest motives which
can influence a true Christian. At one moment
the selfishness and irritability of the sufferers
require a strong control; at another time their
dejection and bodily weakness require the
utmost tenderness, sympathy, and judgment.
To rebuke the self-righteous, to bind up the
broken-hearted, to strengthen, to comfort the
feeble, to drop the words of peace into the
disturbed or softened mind just at the right
moment;—there are few nurses who could be
entrusted with such a charge, or be brought
to regard it as a part of their duty: while the
"overworked chaplain," as he is called, in

some of the evidence before me, cannot suffice for all, and pays his visits only at stated times, unless urgently called for.

It was from a consideration of these and other evils, and a comparison of our system with that of the Roman Catholic and Protestant Sisterhoods abroad, that a paper was drawn up and sent round to a number of chaplains, medical men, and governors of hospitals, containing a sketch of the training system adopted in the institutions at Kaiserswerth and elsewhere, and inquiries as to the best means of raising the moral character of hospital nurses by substituting women of a better class, properly instructed, and capable of being at once the delegates of the medical men, the assistants of the chaplain, the comfort, blessing, and support of the poor sufferers to whom they minister.

The answers which this circular elicited, twenty-three in number, are given at length in the little book already referred to,* and very

* "Hospitals and Sisterhoods."

curiously characteristic they are of the state of
feeling and opinion on a most important subject.   They are too long to be read here; but,
however differing in views and in character,
the writers agree almost without exception in
two things, — in allowing the evils complain-
ed of even to their utmost extent, and in their
despair of any remedy.

These letters were published, but no result
followed.   The so-called practical men, clergy
and laity, admired the project, praised the
amiable enthusiasts who advocated it, and
shook their wise heads, just as they had formerly shaken them over theories of education
and plans of juvenile reform.

When Admiral Sir Edward Parry was at
the head of the naval hospital at Haslar, the
necessity for a better order of nurses for his
sick men was forced on his attention.   Perhaps he had heard of the employment of the
Sisters of Charity in the naval hospitals of
France; at all events, the hope of procuring
nurses of a similar character induced him to

draw up a sort of appeal, in which he adverted to the *impossibility* of obtaining any attendance for the hospital inmates, but such as
was of the lowest grade, — such as only "the
most absolute necessity would justify his ad-
mitting into the establishment." The result
was, incalculable evil to the men; who, instead of being elevated and softened by suffering and seclusion, were morally lowered
and hardened by contact with coarse and
immoral women, even at the very moment
when all that was best and manliest within
them ought to have been wakened up and
appealed to; and most earnestly he solicited
the aid of all good Christians to induce three
or four respectable women to volunteer their
services and to undergo an especial training,
such as had been adopted at Kaiserswerth;
then to superintend others, and thus to help
him in his earnest endeavor to raise the moral
tone of one of the most important of our
national hospitals. The paper was signed by
five medical officers, and circulated extensive-
ly. It did not elicit a single offer. " I confess," said Sir Edward, commenting with

some sadness on his complete failure, " I have never been able to arrive at any definite or satisfactory conclusion as to the best mode of meeting the requirements of a Protestant community." *

Let us contrast this with Kaiserswerth, — a Protestant institution, be it remembered. An appeal being made in 1853, that more voluntary nurses were wanting in the hospitals, it was answered by one hundred and fifty applicants, of whom seventy were accepted and put under a course of instruction.

One fact more. The Bishop of London publicly expressed his regrets that he had seen, one after another, all the plans for this object fail utterly. As to the reason for it, he seemed as much at a loss as Sir Edward Parry.

It would have been said, in truth, but a few weeks ago, that no cause *could* be more hopeless, than that which I am now advocating. The obstacle seemed to consist, not

* " Hospitals and Sisterhoods," p. 41.

in the want of charity, but in the want of
moral courage and the most obtuse ignorance.
Opinions are believed in simply because they
are echoed round us.   The conscience is trained to obey the pressure of an exterior force,
rather than trust to the promptings of an internal impulse; and the convictions and the
will of a generous and powerful individual
nature sink into inertness for want of self-
reliance. How many women, widows, and
unmarried of a certain age, would have gladly
responded to the appeal from Haslar Hospital,
if ignorance, timidity, a defective education,
and a terror of the vulgar, stupid prejudices
around them, — chiefly, I am ashamed to say,
masculine prejudices, — had not stifled their
natural feelings and trammelled their natural
energies! True, hundreds of women had done
the same thing before ; but then those were
Nuns and Roman Catholics, — words of fear!
— precedents to be repudiated! — snares forg-
ed by Satan himself in guise of philanthropy!
Thus the women had no moral courage for
themselves.   On the part of the men — (and
no combined efforts of women can possibly

succeed or come to good without the co-
operation and guidance of men) — there was
an absurd horror of all innovation; want of
confidence in the material to be employed;
want of talent and influence to organize it.

Every one admitted, as a natural law, an
undeniable truth, that early education and the
nursing of the sick belong especially to the
women. Every one admitted the great, the
almost insuperable difficulty of finding women competent to educate, or competent to
nurse. To furnish them with the means of
acquiring skill and competency in their own
department of work has never been regarded
as the duty, the business, the interest of our
pastors and masters; while, with a strange
injustice, the want of such skill and competency has been a perpetual source of complaint and ridicule. The education commonly
given to a boy makes him, at least, a brave
man; a man who can fight till he falls. Does
the education given to a woman make her a
brave woman? Yet how every man feels the
value of those words, " A brave woman!" —

a woman who knows how to act in difficulties, how to endure in suffering, how to be faithful to a trust, and can speak the truth without fear and without disguise. A woman should be a brave woman who aspires to please a brave man!

Whatsoever things are good, whatsoever things are wise, whatsoever things are holy, must be accomplished by communion between brave men and brave women. The work must be shared between them, or it will perish and fail utterly. Yet up to this moment you will find men and women working separately. You will observe that all legislation takes for granted that men and women are to be an everlasting cause of mutual mischief wherever combined; and always *supposes* an antagonistic position if they are separated. The most humane and recent laws aspire no farther than to defend the women from being beaten to death, and this because all legislation is derived from the old Pagan law, or the old monkish prejudices. These barbarous, and stupid, and irreligious notions have caused the evil they supposed, and incalculable has been the amount of sin and misery springing from them.

Not for ever, certainly, — but for how long a period, who can tell? — such miserable obstacles might have continued to limit, to perplex, to paralyze the aspirations of the wise and benevolent, if a crisis had not come, and if that crisis had not found among us a man with sufficient faith and courage to break down the barriers of routine; and a woman generous and gentle, and gifted with sufficient energy to act out "the plan which pleased her childish thought," * and prepared, by education and habit, as well as by a rare combination of the sympathetic and administrative faculties, to do so. Nothing could more strongly exhibit the perplexed state of feeling and opinion in this country, on some momentous points, than the manner in which Mr. Sidney Herbert's proposal to send off a staff

* " It is the generous spirit, who when brought
   Among the tasks of real life hath wrought
   Upon the plan which pleased his childish thought."
                                    Wordsworth.

of voluntary female nurses to our hospitals in the East, and Miss Nightingale's consent to place herself at the head of them, were received by the people, and commented on by the newspapers. There was, indeed, a genuine spontaneous burst of admiration from the public heart, mixed up, however, with fear, with incredulity, with amazement; as if it were a thing unheard of, unknown, and now for the first time attempted, that women of refined habits, and holding a certain position in society, should, from motives of piety and humanity, become nurses in a hospital.*

* " When, at the commencement of the war, the practice of the French to employ female nurses in their hospitals was spoken of, the opinion of the medical men and of the medical department was given against the employment of female nurses. I did not feel myself at liberty to act at variance with that opinion and the experience on which it was founded, although I now feel that that experience was based upon a totally different state of things, and that those opinions were formed upon circumstances which did not resemble the present. The reason why in former times nurses were found unsuited to the care of English soldiers was because the women selected for that service were not, as now, women of education and of pious feelings, who volunteered their services, but women hired for the service, who, both abroad and at home, grew callous, and manifested a harshness and want of sympathy with the sufferers that rendered them unfit for the due performance of their duties. But hardly any other

" Common-sense" styled them *romantic*, a convenient epithet, by which the worldly-minded set the seal of reprobation on anything which steps beyond the bounds of conventionalism, — as if all that is really great and good in humanity were to be kept for fiction and poetry, and only its futilities and frivolities acted out into realities! And " sentiment," with that squeamishness in regard to manners and latitude in regard to morals, which characterize certain classes of society, stigmatized the whole arrangement as " unfe-

ladies had given a fairer trial to the present system than the one who has so nobly volunteered to go to the hospital at Scutari. I believe that the names of Miss Nightingale and of those ladies who have stepped forward in the cause of Christian love will be handed down to posterity in company with those of the gallant men who have been wounded in the service of their country. They have left a comfortable, and in many instances a luxurious home, for the purpose of adopting a profession which is most distasteful to many women of delicate minds, in the hope of assuaging the sufferings of our gallant fellows, and of fulfilling a Christian duty. I believe that through the instrumentality of these ladies more will be done to reëstablish the efficiency of our hospital establishments, than has ever been done by the medical men themselves, although there never have been greater exertions, greater self-denial, or greater zeal, shown by the members of that profession." — (*Speech of the Duke of Newcastle, Dec.* 12, 1854)

minine,"— another word of most convenient
misapplication. The most hopeful and liberal
minded were troubled by a vision of a hundred enthusiastic sentimental women rushing
off to Scutari, and on their arrival there falling
into hysterics;— of " hard-headed Scotch surgeons," wrathfully aghast at the invasion of
their domains by impertinent femalities. Then
there was the mockery of the light-minded;
the atrocious innuendo of the dissolute ; the
sneer of the ignorant; the scepticism of the
cold. I have seen men, who deem it quite a
natural and necessary thing that a woman,—
some women at least,— should lead the life of
a courtesan, put on a look of offended propriety at the idea of a woman nursing a sick
soldier. I have seen men, ay, and women
too, who deem it a matter of course that our
streets should be haunted by contagious vice,
disgusted by the idea of women turning
apothecaries and hospitalières. And worse
than all, I have heard men and women too,
who acknowledge the teaching of Christ, who
call themselves by his name, who believe in
his mission of mercy, disputing about the exact

shade of orthodoxy in a woman who had
offered up every faculty of her being at the
feet of her Redeemer!

On the other hand, people were heard con-
gratulating each other on "the lucky chance"
that a Miss Nightingale should have been
forth-coming just at the moment she was
wanted. Suppose there had been no Miss
Nightingale at once able and willing to do the
work, — no woman in a position which gave
her social influence to overcome the obstacles
of custom and prejudice, — suppose that the
example of noble courage and devotion which
led the way for others had been wanting, —
is every crisis of danger, distress, and difficulty
involving human life, human suffering, human
interests of the deepest consequence, to find
us at the mercy of " a lucky chance?" — at
the mercy of people who have never thought
seriously on any great question, or taken the
trouble to make up their minds one way or
another? I trust that England has many
daughters not unworthy of being named with
Florence Nightingale; as quick in sympathy,

as calm in judgment, as firm in duty, as awake
to charity; but the ability, the acquirements,
the experience, the tact, the skill in judging
and managing character, and overcoming adverse circumstances, at which ministers and
officials were filled with wonder, — were these
matters of chance? They were the result of
years of study, of patient observation, of severe
training. In what school? In none that
England affords to her daughters; *this* is the
wonder!

Even in the applause, — the sort of glorifi-
cation, — which has followed on the success
of this experiment, there has been something
to sadden and humiliate a thinking and feeling
mind. There has been perpetual reiteration
of *astonishment* at the magnanimity of those
who had quitted a comfortable, and in some
cases a luxurious home, and all the pleasures
of a refined and intellectual existence, " to
assuage the sufferings of our gallant country-
men, and to perform a sacred and sublime
duty ;" as if to assuage suffering and to prefer
a sacred and sublime duty to the temptations

of leisure or pleasure, were not the woman's province and privilege as well as the man's; as if the same thing had never been done before in past times and other creeds; as if in these present times we had not known women who, in the midst of all the splendor of a luxurious home, have perished by a slow wasting disease of body and mind, because they had nothing to do, — no sphere of activity commensurate with the large mental powers or passionate energy of character with which God had endowed them. Send such a woman to her piano, her books, her cross-stitch; she answers you with *despair!* But send her on some mission of mercy, send her where she may perhaps die by inches in achieving good for others, and the whole spirit rises up strong and rejoicing.*

*. One of the ladies of Scutari, rich, well-born, and accomplished, on being informed that she had been selected as one of those who were to be sent to a post where additional difficulty, suffering, and even danger awaited her, clasped her hands and uttered a fervent " Thank God ! "

I remember a Sister of Charity who had been sent off at half an hour's notice to a district where the cholera was raging among the most squalid and miserable poor, and I never shall forget the look of radiant happiness and thankfulness on that face.

I am anxious on this point not to be misunderstood. If you speak to some people of
the necessity of finding better and higher employment for women, they inquire merrily
how you would like a female house of parliament? or they congratulate themselves that
ladies are not likely to act as constables, or to
be drawn for the militia. Thus they would
put down one of the most terribly momentous
questions that has ever occupied the thoughts
of thoughtful men, — a question which is at
the very core of social morals: but none who
now listen to me would, I think, condescend
to such cruel and absurd wit.

Then, again, an intelligent and amiable man
will say: — " It is all very well; but I should
not like my daughter to do so-and-so." But
the question is not what this or that individual would choose his daughter to do. It
remains with him to settle this within the
precincts of his family; only it is most unjust
to make his particular feelings and opinions
the rule of life for others, without once
approaching the question as one of social

morals, as one of justice and humanity; without once reflecting that all the unemployed
and superfluous women in England cannot be
sempstresses, governesses, and artists.   Why
is it that we see so many women carefully
educated going over to the Roman Catholic
Church?   For no other reason but for the
power it gives them to throw their energies
into a sphere of definite utility under the control of a high religious responsibility.   What
has been done by our sisters of the Roman
Catholic Church, can it not be accomplished
in a religion which does not aim to subjugate,
but to direct the will?   What has been done
under the hardest despotisms, and recognized
in the midst of the wildest excesses of de-
mocracy, can it not be done under a political
system which disdains to use the best and
highest faculties of our nature in a spirit of
calculation, or in furtherance of the purposes
of a hierarchy or an oligarchy, — which boasts
its equal laws and equal rights, and is at
this moment ruled by a gentle-hearted, noble-
minded woman?

With regard to this present experiment, (if that can be called an experiment which the experience of a thousand years had established as a principle,) it seems to have succeeded beyond all hope, and its success has demonstrated the deep-lying wisdom of what was at first a mere expedient adopted for a passing difficulty. Henceforth the name of Florence Nightingale is dear and familiar in our households, — women glory in her, men rise up and call her blessed. " I have received," said Mr. Sidney Herbert, speaking from his place in Parliament, " not only from medical men, but from many others who have had an opportunity of making observations, letters couched in the highest possible terms of praise. I will not repeat the words, but no higher words of praise could be applied to women, for the wonderful energy, the wonderful tact, the wonderful tenderness, combined with the extraordinary self-devotion which have been displayed by Miss Nightingale ; and I am glad to say that the characteristics which have been shown by that lady, the force and

influence of her character, seem to have pene-
trated all those working with her, and I
believe, not only the patients themselves, but
every person connected with the hospital, will
be benefited by the admixture of this new
element in the management of a military
hospital." It will extend yet farther, as I
hope and believe; to results incalculable and
certainly not contemplated, when that band
of sisters, accompanied by tears, prayers, and
blessings, departed from our shores to the far
East. We are told of the burst of gratitude
with which they were received. " Now we
know that our country cares for us!" was the
exclamation of one of the poor fellows. I do
not think it right to tell here all I *could* tell
on the subject of these excellent and high-
hearted women, all the difficulties they have
had to contend with and have surmounted,
all the feelings they have awakened of gratitude and veneration; of death-beds comforted
and hallowed, of wandering and distempered
spirits recalled and healed — no — I cannot!
it is all too sacred and too present to us to be
spoken of yet; — nor should I feel justified in

repeating what has been privately and confidentially communicated. What has been published in the newspapers has probably been read and re-read with hearts burning within them, by every one now listening to me; — but one or two passages in reference to the general good effected, I may be allowed to cite.

Mr. Stafford, in his attack on the late ministry, made at least one especial exception to their misdeeds, — on one point he gave to Mr. Sidney Herbert most deserved praise. " He congratulated the Secretary at War on the sending out of the female nurses last autumn. Success more complete had never attended human efforts, than that which had resulted from this excellent measure. They could scarcely realize, without personally seeing it, the heartfelt gratitude of the soldiers to these noble ladies, or the amount of misery they had relieved, or the degree of comfort, — he might say of joy, — they had diffused; and it was impossible to do justice, not only to the kindness of heart, but to the clever judgment,

ready intelligence, and experience displayed
by the distinguished lady to whom this diffi-.
cult mission had been intrusted. If Scutari
was not altogether as we could wish it to
be, it was because of the inadequate powers
confided to Miss Nightingale; and if the
Government did not stand by her and her
devoted band, and repel unfounded and un-
generous attacks made upon them, — if it did
not consult their wishes and yield to their superior judgment in many respects, — it would
deserve the execration of the public." Strong
language this! but excusable from one who
spoke with glowing heart of what he had
seen! — listened to with sympathy, and responded to with cheers by generous men and
gentlemen.

Another speaker on the same side expresses
his belief that even the mere presence and
superintendence of gentle well-educated women would be morally beneficial. I recollect
that it was said at first, that not only the
medical attendants but the sick and suffering
would be quite uncomfortably "embarrassed"

by this innovation; but if a cessation of coarse
language, if better feelings, if more self-control, arise from patients and orderlies being
" embarrassed " by the presence and ministra-
tion of superior women, I conceive that it will
not be an evil but a benefit, and one that will
not, in all cases, cease with the hour of suffering. We may at least hope that a man who
has been thus tended by gentle and superior
beings of the other sex, will hardly be so ready
as heretofore to make women the victims of
his levity or brutality; what he did not spare
for the sake of mother or sister, he may perhaps, in some hour of temptation and selfish
impulse, spare for the sake of those who bent
over him when "pain and anguish wrung the
brow," and whispered low the solemn words
of peace, of patience, of divine hope and
comfort, while laying the pillow under a poor
fellow's rough head, or holding the cup to his
parched lips. As woman, even because she *is*
woman, feels all the healing and strengthening power which lies in the man's mind, and
in cases of severe physical or moral suffering,
throws herself with almost helpless confi-

dence on her priest or her physician, — so it is with man : — he softens under the influence of a softer nature, he confesses a healing power in the organism which was created thus to refresh, restore, and purify his own, and yields to woman where he would not yield to one of his own sex. This I believe to be a simple universal physiological law, not yet recognized in all its bearings. To borrow a happy illustration from Mr. Macaulay, — he asks, somewhere, " In how many months would the first human beings who settled on the shores of the ocean have been justified in believing that the moon had an influence on the tides ?" and I may ask, for how many more centuries shall we stand on the shores of the great ocean of life without knowing under what near or remote mysterious influences its floods rise or fall, are moved to disturbance or hushed to tranquillity ?

I am acquainted with an army surgeon whose regiment, a few years since, was ordered to India. Almost immediately on landing, numbers of the men were attacked by cholera.

They were prostrated one after another, — sank, — died, almost as much from terror and despair as from the disease itself. As the senior surgeon, my friend felt deeply his responsibility, — as a humane man he felt for the suffering of his men. He had exhausted all the resources of his art, but the disease was spreading fearfully. One morning, on coming home to his wife, after visiting the hospital, he said, " I don't know what to do with my poor fellows, — they wring my very heart, — they are dying of faint-heartedness as much as anything else!" " Suppose," said she, " I were to go and see them, — would it do any good?" " Well," he replied, with tears in his eyes, " I should not have asked it of you, but, as you offer it, I think it *would* do good." She threw on her dressing-gown, and repaired at once to the hospital. Leaning on her husband's arm, she walked through the wards where the sick and dying lay crowded together ; — she spoke kind and cheerful words to those who could hear her, and they seemed to revive under the influence of her presence. She continued her visits daily. The most despairing took comfort, men whose condition seemed hopeless recovered. They thought, they even said, " It is not so bad with us if *she* can come among us!" They watched for her coming, and received her, when she came, with blessings : and the ravages of the disease were from that time allayed. Now there is nothing extraordinary in all this; hundreds of such instances might be recorded; some example of the kind will probably start into the recollection of many who listen to me; but such facts have never been brought together, and considered in the abstract as illustrating a principle, or as substantiating a truth, — a most important principle, and a most vital truth ; they remain, consequently, isolated facts, strongly exciting our sympathy and interest ; and nothing more.

I have met with Protestant Sisters of Charity, — very many, — who did not assume that name for themselves. I will mention one instance. She was a lady, a foreigner, not merely of good birth, but of high and titled rank. She had begun life in a court; she had been *dame d'honneur* to a brilliant princess. Certain events, on which I have no right to dwell, clouded her youth, and gave her the wish to devote herself wholly to the service of the wretched. She consulted a well-known physician, who looked upon her resolve as a mere fit of excitement, and reasoned strongly against it. Finding this in vain, he thought to shock her delicate nerves by assigning to her at first some of the most trying, most revolting duties of a hospital. The effect was the reverse of what he had expected. The near spectacle of suffering which she had power to aid and alleviate, the perception of certain evils she might have the power to reform or at least ameliorate, only made her more resolved, and she quietly took her vocation upon her and pursued it steadily. The first time I saw this lady she was seated in the garden of a mutual friend. It was a beautiful summer evening; she had finished her day's work, and her later duties had not commenced. She was sitting on a bench knitting, with a cup of coffee beside her, dressed with great simplicity, but without peculiarity; her face was grave, but when she looked up to speak it brightened into a ready smile. She had at that time pursued her vocation, unfaltering in courage and perseverance, for sixteen years; she had introduced, as I was told, many salutary reforms into the hospitals she had attended, and exercised, wherever she went, a beneficent influence.

Mr. Sidney Herbert, in requesting the assistance of Miss Nightingale, after using some arguments drawn even from that task " full of horror " to which he invited her, — arguments which no woman at once capable and tenderhearted could have resisted, — alludes to more remote but probable results following on her conduct. He says truly: — " If this succeed, an enormous amount of good will be done now, and to persons deserving everything at our hands; and a prejudice will be broken through and a precedent established which will multiply the good to all time."

No doubt; but it will be through the pa-

tience, faith, and wisdom of men and women
working together. In an undertaking so wholly
new to our English customs, so much at variance with the usual education given to women
in this country, we shall meet with perplexities,
difficulties, even failures. All the ladies who
have gone to Scutari may not turn out heroines.
There may be vain babblings and scribblings
and indiscretions, such as may put weapons
into adverse hands. The inferior and paid
nurses may, some of them, have carried to
Scutari bad habits arising from imperfect
training. Still let us trust that a *principle*
will be recognized in this country which will
not be again lost sight of. It will be the true,
the lasting glory of Florence Nightingale and
her band of devoted assistants, that they have
broken through what Goethe calls a " Chinese
wall of prejudices;" prejudices religious, social, professional; and established a precedent
which will indeed " multiply the good to all
time." No doubt there are hundreds of women
who would now gladly seize the privileges held
out to them by such an example, and crowd
to offer their services: but would they pay

the price for such dear and high privileges? Would they fit themselves duly for the performance of such services, and earn, by distasteful and even painful studies, the necessary certificates for skill and capacity? Would they, like Miss Nightingale, go through a seven years' probation, to try at once the steadiness of their motives and the steadiness of their nerves? Such a trial is absolutely necessary, for hundreds of women will fall into the common error of mistaking an impulse for a vocation. But I do believe that there are also hundreds who are fitted, or would gladly, at any self-sacrifice, fit themselves, for the work, if the means of doing so were allowed to them. At present an English lady has no facilities whatever for obtaining the information or experience required; no such institutions are open to her, and yet she is ridiculed for presenting herself without the competent knowledge! This seems hardly just.

The horrors of war which have called forth so noble a display of the best capabilities of women, are accidents in the world's history;

but the capabilities so called forth are not accidental, nor will they cease with the occasion. They are intrinsic and essential and ever at hand, though hidden under a mass of cruel conventionalities, like those precious drugs and medicaments, which, as we are told, were stowed away under heaps of shell, shot, and gunpowder. Having once discovered their treasures, men have now to use them. War will cease, but here at home, the need of women's active intelligence and tenderness to alleviate a mass of social evils, will not cease. The time is surely coming when we shall know how to apply such material better than we have yet done. The time is surely coming when private charity will not be so often desultory, capricious, misdirected, meddlesome, and unwelcome ; when public charity will not be worked like a steam power, through mere official mechanism, but by human sympathies, cheerful, wise, and tender. The contributions poured into the magistrates' poor-box on every public appeal, the distribution of blankets and flannels, and soup, and all creature comforts, are in themselves things excellent and seasonable, and worthy of all imitation; but should this be the only intercourse between those who give and those who want? — those who pity and those who suffer? The love that works for our good should elicit love in return, or it is nothing but a machine. Such is not God's love to us, whose highest benefit it is that it awakens our responsive love for him, and makes us better through that love. Should we not also endeavor to make our fellow-creatures better through our charity, to touch the nature and make it respond to our own, till there shall be more of mutual faith and comprehension, as well as a more diffused sympathy through the different orders of society?

An institution such as I have in my mind, should be a place where women could obtain a sort of professional education under professors of the other sex, — for men are the best instructors of women; — where they might be trained as hospital and village nurses, visitors of the poor, and teachers in the elementary and reformatory schools; so that a certain

number of women should always be found
ready and competent to undertake such work
in our public charitable and educational institutions as should be fitted for them ; — I say
fitted for them, and for which by individual
capacity and inclination they should be *fitted*,
and that corresponding fitness tested by a
rather lengthened probation and a strict examination.   It seems rather unjust to sneer at a
woman's unfitness for certain high duties,
domestic and social, unless the possibility of
obtaining better instruction be afforded.   All
the unmarried and widowed women of the
working classes cannot be sempstresses and
governesses ; nor can all the unmarried women
of the higher classes find in society and visiting, literature and art, the purpose, end, and
aim of their existence.   We have works of
love and mercy for the best of our women to
do, in our prisons and hospitals, our reformatory schools, and I will add our workhouses; *

* "A principal reason of the cleanliness and order of the
workhouses in Holland, is the attention and humanity of the
governesses, for each house has four, who take charge of the
inspection, and have their names painted in the room." —
(*Howard on Prisons*, 3d edit. 1784, p. 48.)

"The workhouses at Amsterdam were under the direction

but then we must have them such as we want them, — not impelled by transient feelings, but by deep abiding motives, — not amateur *ladies* of charity, but brave women, whose vocation is fixed, and whose faculties of every kind have been trained and disciplined to their work under competent instruction from men, and tested by a long probation.

It will be said, perhaps, that when you thus train a woman's instinctive feelings of pity and tenderness for a particular purpose, to act under control and in concert with others, you

of six regents (governors) and four governesses, who appointed under them two ' fathers,' and two ' mothers,' (overseers), whose business it was to superintend the work, diet, and lodging of the inmates," &c. (p. 59.)

" The regents (*i. e.*, governors of the houses of correction) have a room in which they assemble once a fortnight. Their ladies assemble in another room to give directions concerning the week's linen, provisions, &c.

" They (the governesses) also attend by rotation at dinner and at other times, and their accounts are carried to the regents."

In these days the *order* and *cleanliness* which Howard so admired are not wanting in our workhouses; but some elements *are* wanting, such as judicious and refined and truly religious and kind-hearted women would alone supply.

[Since the above note was written I have received a very benevolent and sensible letter on the subject of female supervision in workhouses, which I am sorry I cannot insert here.]

take away their spontaneousness, their grace, even in some sort their sincerity ; consequently their power to work good. This is like the reasoning of my Uncle Toby, who, in describing the Béguines, says, " They visit and take care of the sick by profession ; but I had rather, for my own part, that they did it out of good nature." Would Uncle Toby have admitted the necessary inference, — namely, that when you train and discipline a man to be a soldier, to serve in the ranks, and obey orders under pain of being shot, you take away his valor, his manly strength, his power to use his weapon? We know it is not so. Never yet did the sense of duty diminish the force of one generous impulse in man or woman!— that sublimest of bonds, when in harmony with our true instincts, intensifies while it directs them.

There are many other objections and obstacles, lying in our onward path, of which I cannot dissemble the magnitude. There is in this country a sort of scrupulousness about interfering with the individual will, which renders it peculiarly difficult to make numbers work together unless disciplined as you would discipline a regiment. The obvious want of discipline and organization in our civil service, has been a source of difficulties, and even of fatal mistakes in the commencement of this war. In any community of reasonable beings, therefore in any community of women, as of men, there must be gradations of capacity,* and difference of work.

* " Many years ago, during a residence in Warrington, — at that period the seat of a number of branches of industry demanding artistic skill, as the manufacture of flint glass, of files, and of all kinds of tools, — when sitting one night by the fire of a tool-maker, I was struck by the beauty of the small files, vices, and other tools used in watch-making. Knowing that he employed apprentices, I asked if he found that they all had the steady patience, the clearness of sight, and delicacy of hand required for such work; to which he replied, that not half attained the skill to qualify them, at the end of their term, for journeymen; that some gave up the attempt to learn the branch, and went to another; that others, who completed their apprenticeship, if they remained, got employment only when trade was brisk; when it was slack they were the first to be discharged; whilst others, again, became laborers, that is, *served* the skilful hands.

" I next inquired of a glass manufacturer, himself originally a workman, what proportion, apprenticed to the flint-glass making, were worth retaining as journeymen; when he replied : — ' Out of ten apprenticed, not three proved good hands; the others mostly fall to the lower branches, as tending the

To make or require vows of obedience is
objectionable; yet we know that the voluntary

furnaces and the like; a certain number, too, are retained in
the place of boys, that is, as the glass-blowers' assistants : but
when fresh apprentice lads are taken, or when trade is slack,
these inferior hands are sure to be dismissed.' In respect to
glass-cutting, he said, that probably not half the apprentices
turn out expert; that they drop away out of the branch; but he
was unable to say to what else they betook themselves. With
the same object I continued, in subsequent years, to inquire of
master shoemakers, tailors, letter-press printers, bookbinders,
and of masters in other trades demanding dexterity and skill,
and have found that a considerable proportion of those put to
acquire such branches either fail to do so and drop lower, or
they remain in them and are known by the name of *botchers.*
In this way the descent of numbers in every trade goes on
continually, and shows an inequality in mankind, as to tal-
ents, that will ever baffle the hopes of those enthusiastic
reformers who, in their schemes, or rather dreams, of social
improvement, overlook this natural diversity, and who would
regard all the individuals composing the laboring class as
entitled to share in the fruits of labor.'' — '' I refer to *natural*
inequality, for which there is no help, — as distinguished
from *culpable* inequality, the effect of evil passions and
tempers which generate habits injurious or even completely
obstructive to success in life.'' — (*On Municipal Government.*)

A wisely organized system of work, — intellectual and
moral as well as mechanical work, — provides for this *natural* inequality, and does not place human beings in positions
which they are *naturally* unable to fill with advantage to
themselves or others; and that would be a strange law which
should oblige a master manufacturer to employ *botchers* in
the place of skilled workmen because they present themselves,
and because they also have a right to live by their work.

nurses who went to the East were called upon
to do what comes to the same thing, — to
sign an engagement to obey implicitly a controlling and administrative power, — or the
whole undertaking must have fallen to the
ground. Then, again, questions about costume have been mooted which appear to me
wonderfully absurd. It has been suggested
that there should be something of a unifor-
mity and fitness in the dress worn when on
duty, and this seems but reasonable. I recollect once seeing a lady in a gay light muslin
dress, with three or four flounces, and roses
under her bonnet, going forth to visit her sick
poor. The incongruity struck the mind pain-
fully, — not merely as an incongruity, but as
an impropriety, like a soldier going to the
trenches in opera hat and laced ruffles. Such
follies, arising from individual obtuseness,
must be met by regulations dictated by good
sense, and submitted to as a matter of necessity and obligation.

But it is not my intention to go into any
of these minor points of discipline and ques-

tions of detail. One great object has been
achieved, — a principle has been admitted,
a precedent has been established, of female
labor organized for noble purposes of public
utility, approved by public opinion, guided
and assisted by man's more comprehensive
intellect, sustained and sanctioned by the
authority of the ruling powers. All schemes
for the public good, in which men and women
do not work in communion, have in them the
seeds of change, discord, and decay. Some
time ago Miss Bremer (the Swedish author-
ess) planned a sort of universal feminine
coalition, — a sort of female corresponding
society for sundry pious and charitable purposes. Her plan virtually excluded the co-
operation of the masculine brain, thus dividing
what Nature herself has decreed should never
be disunited without mischief, the element of
power and the element of *love*. The idea was
simply absurd and necessarily impracticable.
Such an association of one half of the human
species in an attitude of independence as regards the other, would have excited a spirit
of antagonism in the men; and among the

women, would have speedily degenerated into a gossiping, scribbling, stitching community, unstable as water; and nothing more need be said of it here, except that it fully deserved the witty rebuke it met with, though not solely nor chiefly on the alleged grounds.

And now I may leave the question at the point to which I have brought it. I will only add that the history of the past, of the possible, of the actually accomplished, which I have here rapidly sketched out, should give us courage in the present and hope for the future.

It is a subject of reproach that in this Christendom of ours, the theory of good which we preach should be so far in advance of our practice; but that which provokes the sneer of the skeptic and almost kills faith in the sufferer, lifts up the contemplative mind with hope. Man's *theory* of good is God's *reality;* man's experience, is the degree to which he has already worked out, in his human capacity, that divine reality. Therefore, whatever our practice may be, let us hold fast to our theories of possible good; let us at least, however they outrun our present powers, keep them in sight, and then our formal lagging practice may in time overtake them. In social morals as well as in physical truths, " The goal of yesterday will be the starting-point of to-morrow;" and the things before which all England now stands in admiring wonder will become "the simple produce of the common day." Thus we hope and believe.

THE

COMMUNION OF LABOR:

A SECOND LECTURE

ON THE

SOCIAL EMPLOYMENTS OF WOMEN

> " —— At last
> She rose upon a wind of prophecy,
> Dilating on the future : — ' Everywhere
> Two heads in council ; two beside the hearth,
> Two in the tangled business of the world,
> Two in the liberal offices of life.' "
>
> TENNYSON.

PREFACE

TO THE SECOND EDITION.

A second Edition of this little lecture, (or essay, for I hardly know which to call it,) being required within the short period of a month, I seize the opportunity to add a few words to the preface already printed.

The reception, altogether unexpected, which the principles here so briefly and so imperfectly announced have met with, I certainly do not take to be any testimony to the merit of the book, as such, but rather as a proof that it has struck upon a chord of feeling in the public mind, tuned and ready to vibrate to the most unpractised touch. So unlooked-for, indeed, has been the general expression of responsive sympathy, public and private, that the hand laid thus timidly and unskilfully upon the chords, almost " recoils from the sound itself hath made."

Not less have I been touched with pleasure and surprise by the numerous communications

in the present state of society, imperatively demanded.

This Lecture, having been delivered orally to a circle of friends, has unconsciously assumed a somewhat egotistical tone and form, which the reader is entreated kindly to excuse, and to remember that its intention is not to dictate, but merely to suggest.

August 17, 1856.

CONTENTS.

THE COMMUNION OF LABOR:

A SECOND LECTURE ON THE SOCIAL EMPLOY-
MENTS OF WOMEN.

(Delivered privately June 28th, 1856, and printed by desire.)

It is nearly a year and a half since my friends gathered round me and listened very kindly and patiently to certain suggestions relative to the social employments of women, more especially as "Sisters of Charity, at home and abroad." The views I then advocated had been long in my mind: but great events, at that time recent, and coming home to all hearts, had rendered the exposition of those views more seaonable, more interesting, perhaps also more intelligible, than they would otherwise have been.

The publication of that Lecture having attracted more attention than I had reason to expect, and having given rise to some discussion, public and private, I have been advised, and have taken courage, once more, and probably for the last time, to recur to the same subject. It is a subject which, if it be worth any attention whatever, is worth the most serious and solemn consideration; for it concerns no transient, no partial interest, lying on the surface of life, but rather the very stuff of which life is made. Some new observations, some additional facts, I have to communicate, which, while they illustrate the principles laid down in my former Lecture, will, I hope, add force to my arguments. These observations, these facts, will not at once overcome all objections, will not in the first instance meet with any thing like general acceptance; but they will perhaps open up new sources of thought; and if thought lead to inquiry, and inquiry lead to conviction — for or against — I should be content to abide that issue.

The questions as yet unsettled seem to be these: —

Whether a more enlarged sphere of social work may not be allowed to woman in perfect

accordance with the truest feminine instincts ?
Whether there be not a possibility of her sharing practically in the responsibilities of social
as well as domestic life ?   Whether she might
not be better prepared to meet and exercise
such higher responsibilities ?   And whether
such a communion of labor might not lead to
the more humane ordering of many of our
public institutions, to a purer standard of
morals, to a better mutual comprehension and
a finer harmony between men and women,
when thus called upon to work together, and
(in combining what is best in the two natures)
becoming what God intended them to be, the
supplement to each other ?

Let it not be supposed that I am about to
enter an arena of public strife.   For any truth
in which I believe, I could suffer — no matter
what — or die if need were, yet feel that I
could scarcely strike a blow, far less inflict a
wound.   Conflict, which rouses up the best
and highest powers in some characters, in
others not only jars the whole being, but par-
alzyes the faculties.   This, of course, is a mere

matter of individual temperament; yet, on the whole, in looking back to the history of human progress, I doubt whether any great truth was ever much advanced by conflict, still less by compromise. The hardest battle ever fought for truth left some doubt as to which side had the advantage ; and those who have conceded or sacrificed some portion of the truth by way of securing some other portion (a favorite expedient with politicians who call themselves practical), have not, I think, been successful in their piecemeal morality, or their piecemeal legislation. Let us accept gratefully some portion of what we believe to be just, if we cannot yet obtain the whole; but that is quite different from conceding any portion of a principle. We shall, meantime, do well to take our stand on the highest point we can attain to, beyond the reach of the tempest and the conflict which agitate the waves of fashion and opinion. At last, the rising flood will bring to our side those who have been swimming with the current or struggling in the turmoil; catching at every stray fragment of popular doctrine which floated past them at the level of their eye, and holding it up as if they had rescued from the deep some priceless truth. These deceptions they have dropped one by one, and now we have them beside us: they have planted their foot where we have planted ours. We are no longer lonely, and we have been ever at peace with ourselves and others; seemingly passive to falsehood, but in reality steadfast in faith; — and this is better than strife.

But ere I proceed farther, there is one point on which I am anxious not to be misunderstood, one consideration which I am desirous to place on its true grounds in reference to my present subject, — the social position and occupations of women.

"Gagnez les femmes," said one of the acutest of modern politicians when giving his last instructions to an ambassador. "We write in vain if we have not the women on our side," said one of the poets of our own time; and we women know full well that we must think, and write, and speak in vain without the sanction of the manly intellect, — without the sympathy of the manly heart. At this moment I feel assured of both as I have never felt before.

It ought to give us courage and comfort to know that the laws relating to property and marriage, which have hitherto pressed so heavily on the well-being and happiness of one half of the community, are under the consideration of wise and able men, and may be safely left in their hands. We may have to wait long for those practical measures of justice which are contemplated, but we can afford to wait, now that the injustice has been openly acknowledged by philosophical statesmen and experienced lawyers. There still exist, however, some singular misconceptions, both as to the existing evil and the remedy required; and the expression of opinion and feeling in public and in private which has arisen out of the late discussion of these laws in both Houses of Parliament, has been very curious and conflicting.

We must acknowledge, that a law which should forbid a woman to give all she has to give to the man she loves and trusts, though

to her own perdition, would be certainly a very
foolish and a very useless law. Whether the
concession be from impulse, or devotedness, or
pity, or ignorance, she must abide by her own
act; it must rest on her own conscience. But
the law which punishes, with extreme severity,
the man who takes from her by force what she
desires to withhold, is a just and righteous law.
So, in regard to property, a law which should
interdict the woman from giving all her possessions and earnings, if she chooses, to her
husband, would be a foolish and a useless
law: in this case, as in the other, she must
abide by her own act, and its consequences.
But the law which empowers her husband to
take away all she may possess, or may have
earned by her labor, against her will and to
her destruction, is surely cruel. Again, a law
which should give to the wife the independent
administration of her property, and at the
same time leave her husband responsible for
her debts, would be equally foolish and cruel.
These seem to be clear and simple principles
of justice which will be carried out sooner or
later, though the legal details at this present

time may be complicated by difficulties arising out of existing laws.*

But I must here distinctly explain that, when asked to place my name to a petition against the present marital laws of property, I did so, with no special reference to their practical effect in particular instances, but merely as I would protest against any other manifest injustice, either in regard to men or women, or both. The truth is, that far beyond the palpable, visible working of these laws, cruel as they are in individual cases, lies an infinitely more fatal mischief in their injurious effect on the masses of the people. What matter how such laws act here or there, — how far they are to be excused as expedient, or to be sustained by custom, —

---

* A woman seldom generalizes. Put the question before her, whether a wife should have some control over her own earnings, she exclaims, " Not for the world ! I leave all these things to Fred ; Fred understands money-matters, and accounts, and all that ; and it is such a pleasure to owe everything to him ! " Of course we sympathize with the wife, her Fred standing for all mankind, and her own position for that of all women : meantime how does it fare with her poor working sister in the neighboring alley ? for that also is to be considered.

how easily they may be evaded by one class, though they fall heavily on another? — what signifies all this if they permeate, and in some sort vitiate, the relations of the two sexes throughout the whole community? The direct action of such laws may be confined to the conjugal relation; but the indirect action, as reflected in feeling and opinion, operates on all, married and unmarried. These observations refer merely to their practical effects; but not even those who plead for their expediency in a complex commercial community, where the question of property enters into all relations and contracts, and can hardly be touched without danger or at least disturbance, deny the abstract injustice of such laws. Now every injustice is a form of falsehood, every falsehood accepted and legalized, works in the social system like poison in the physical frame, and may taint the whole body politic through and through, ere we have learned in what quivering nerve or delicate tissue to trace and detect its fatal presence. Human laws which contravene the laws of God, are not laws, but lies; and, like all lies, must perish

in the long run. But there was a saying
of a clever politician, that a lie believed in
but for half an hour might cause a century
of mischief. What then, I would ask, is
likely to be the effect of these laws which
have existed as part of our common law for
centuries past, — laws which may well be
called lies, inasmuch as they suppose a state
of things which has no real existence in the
divine regulation of the world? — laws which
during all that period have tended to degrade
the woman in the eyes of the man, interfered
with the sacredness of the domestic relations,
and infected the whole social system?

I regard the existence of these laws as the
source of especial and fatal mischief. I look
upon them as one cause why it is difficult for
men and women to work together harmoniously; — how can it be otherwise where the
conditions under which they must be associated are, in the first instance, so unequal as
to be almost antagonistic? I look upon these
laws as one cause of prostitution, because, in
so far as they have lowered the social position
of the woman, they have lowered the value of

her labor, and have thus exposed her to want
and temptation, which would not otherwise
have existed.*

Farther, I consider these laws, in so far as
they have influenced the mutual relations of
the two sexes, as one cause of those outrages
on women which are every day brought before
the magistrates, to the disgrace of our civilized
England.

And is it not rather absurd at this time of
day to devise, as an antidote to the working
of these laws, another law, really as unjust in
its way, which punishes a man for ill treating
the creature he has been authorized to regard
as his inferior? Every act of our legislation
which takes for granted antagonism, not
harmony, between the masculine and the
feminine nature, has tended to create that

---

* This at least is the opinion of a man of large experience,
Mr. F. Hill, for many years inspector of prisons. He observes
that the sin and misery alluded to would probably be greatly
diminished " if public opinion no longer upheld the exclusive
spirit by which most of the lucrative employments are restricted to the male sex, whereby the difficulties with which
females have to contend in earning an honest livelihood are
greatly increased."—*Crime, its Amount, Causes, and Remedies, by F. Hill, Inspector of Prisons.*

antagonism. Every act of, our legislature, which, on the one hand, first legalizes wrong, and then, on the other hand, interposes with legal protection against that wrong, must appear to simple, honest minds, a very cruel and clumsy anomaly. By this perpetual, absurd alternation of legalized wrong and legalized vengeance for the wrong, you demoralize relatively both men and women; — the woman in the sight of the man as the licensed victim, the man in the sight of the woman as the chastised tyrant.

I cannot but think that those good men, — prelates, fathers, and lawyers, — who watch over and guard the public morality, and are so fearful lest the harmony and purity of domestic life should suffer by any change in those laws, — I cannot but think them, with submission, mistaken, and that they take but a one-sided and short-sighted view of a most awful subject. I cannot but think that by the abrogation of those laws which have disturbed the divine equilibrium in the relation between the sexes, they would do more for the morality of men and the

protection of women, than by punishing
hundreds of brutal husbands.*

Wise men have doubted whether there

---

* In the North British Review for last June, there is an
excellent article on wife-beating, its causes, and its remedies.
Among the causes adduced, the influence of existing laws on
the morals and the feelings of the lower classes is not expressly mentioned, but it is implied, I think, in the following
passage : —

" Tender, considerate, self-sacrificing, caressing on the one
hand, violent, selfish, brutal on the other, man treats his
helpmate as a child or an invalid, incapable of self-assertion
and self-defence, indeed of all independent action, and therefore an object of deference and attention, to be humored and
indulged, to be aided and supported; or else as an inferior
animal, strong in endurance, to be buffeted, and persecuted,
and outraged, and humiliated, and made to suffer every kind
of wrong. Now, all this doubtless arises from the one
common feeling that woman is the ' weaker vessel.' As is
man's conception of the purposes and uses of strength, so is
his treatment of woman either of a defensive or an offensive
character. In either case, there is an overweening sense of
his own superiority, the practical expression of which, whatever its intent, is degrading to the other sex. We are very
far from any disposition to assert that the two extremes of
defensiveness and offensiveness are equal evils; it may seem,
indeed, to be something of a paradox to place them in the
same category; but they are evils which, though differing in
degree, arise from the same cause and tend to the same
result; both indicate and perpetuate the weakness of woman.
To start from one's seat or rush across a room to pick up a
woman's pocket-handkerchief, or to open a door for her, is a
very different thing from knocking her down and stamping
upon her; but both acts originate in the same sense of man's

ought to be separate laws concerning women,
as such; and scout with reason such phrases
as the *rights of women* and the *wrongs of
women.* I have always had such an intimate
conviction of the absurdity of such phrases,
that I believe I never used them seriously in
my life. In a free country, and a Christian
community, a woman has the rights which
belong to her as a human being, and as a
member of the community, and she has no

superiority, and tend to perpetuate woman's weakness : the
one is a blunder, the other a crime.''

I quite agree with the writer that the substitution of
flogging for imprisonment, as the more immediate and degrading punishment of the two, however well deserved, would
fail in its effect, and that a woman who, under the present
law, makes her complaint with extreme reluctance, under a
law of retaliation will not make it at all : and she is right.
The general impression which exists, that even the women of
the lowest grade will not avail themselves of the protection
of the law under such conditions, shows us the nature of the
creature, though the coarse, the cruel, and the vengeful be
found among them. In fact, the remedy lies deeper than
law can reach. The writer observes, in conclusion : '' What
is wanted indeed most of all, is something that will make it
less a necessity with women to unite themselves legally or
illegally with the other sex. In a large number of cases,
what a woman most looks for in matrimony or concubinage
is a bread-finder. The example is set by the higher classes,
where marriage is looked upon as the end and aim of woman's
life. What else, it is said, can she do ? ''

others. I think it a dangerous and a fatal mistake to legislate on the assumption that there are feminine and masculine rights and wrongs, just as I deem it a fatal error in morals to assume that there are masculine and feminine virtues and vices : there are masculine and feminine *qualities*, wisely and beautifully discriminated, but there are not masculine and feminine virtues and vices. Let us not cheat ourselves by what Mrs. Malaprop would call "a nice derangement of epithets," lest "a nice derangement" of morals ensue thereupon; lest our ideas get hopelessly entangled in words, and our principles of right and wrong become mystified by sentimental phrases.

Nothing in all my experience of life has so shocked me, as the low moral standard of one sex for the other, arising, as I believe, out of this irreligious mistake. I see, among the women of our higher classes, those who have lived much in " the world," as it is called, a sort of mysterious horror of the immorality of men, not as a thing to be resisted, or resented, or remedied, but to be

submitted to as a sort of fatality and necessity (for so it has been instilled into them),
or guarded against by a mere inefficient
barricade of conventional proprieties; while
I see in men of the world a contemptuous
mistrust of women, an impression of their
faithlessness, heartlessness, feebleness, equally
fatal and mistaken.   Men are not all sensual
and selfish; women are not all false and
feeble.   Women, I am sorry to say it, *can*
be sensual and selfish; men *can* be false and
weak; but then I have known men, manly
men, with all the tenderness and refinement
we attribute to women, and I have known
women who have united with all their own
soft sympathies and acute perceptions, quite
a manly strength and sincerity.   The union
is rare; it brings the individual so endowed
near to our ideal of human perfection; it is
what we ought to aim at in all our schemes
of education.   Meantime, let us have what
is the next best thing, the combination of
the two natures, the two influences in all
that we are trying to effect for the good of
the " human family."

I return to the so-called " rights and wrongs of women" only to dismiss them at once from our thoughts and our subject. Morally a woman has a right to the free and entire development· of every faculty which God has given her to be improved and used to His honor. Socially she has a right to the protection of equal laws; the right to labor with her hands the thing that is good; to select the kind of labor which is in harmony with her condition and her powers; to exist, if need be, by her labor, or to profit others by it if she choose. These are her rights, not more nor less than the rights of the man. Let us, therefore, put aside all futile and unreal distinctions. I go back to the principle laid down in my former Lecture, and I appeal against human laws and customs, to the eternal and immutable law of God. When He created all living creatures male and female, was it not His will that out of this very disparity in unity, this likeness in unlikeness, there should· spring an indissoluble bond of mutual attraction and mutual dependence, increasing in degree and durability with every advance of sentient life?

And when He raised *us*, His human creatures, above mere animal existence, did He not make the union, by choice and will, of the man and the woman the basis of all domestic life? all *domestic* life the basis of all social life? all *social* life the basis of all national life? How, then, shall our social and national life be pure and holy, and well ordered before God and man, if the domestic affections and duties be not carried out and expanded, and perfected in the larger social sphere, and in the same spirit of mutual reverence, trust, and kindness which we demand in the primitive relation? It appears to me that when the Creator endowed the two halves of the human race with ever-aspiring hopes, with ever-widening sympathies, with ever-progressing capacities, — when He made them equal in the responsibilities which bind the conscience and in the temptations which mislead the will, — He linked them inseparably in an ever-extending sphere of duties, and an ever-expanding communion of affections ; thus, in one simple, holy, and beautiful ordinance, binding up at once the continuation of the species and its moral, social, and physical progress, through all time.

Let these premises be granted, and hence it follows as a *first* natural and necessary result, and one which the wisest philosophers have admitted, that the relative position of the man and the woman in any community is invariably to be taken as a test of the degree of civilization and well-being in that community. Hence, as a *second* result equally natural and necessary, we find that all that extends and multiplies the innocent relations, the kindly sympathies, the mutual services of men and women, must lead to the happiness and improvement of both. Hence, *thirdly*, if either men or women arrogate to themselves exclusively any of the social work or social privileges which can be performed or exercised perfectly only in communion, they will inevitably fail in their objects, and end probably in corrupting each other. Hence, in conclusion, this last inevitable result; that wherever the nature of either man or woman is, considered as self-dependent or self-sufficing, their rights and wrongs as distinct, their interests

as opposed or even capable of separation,
there we find cruel and unjust laws, discord
and confusion entering into all the forms of
domestic and social life, and the element of
decay in all our institutions. In the midst of
our apparent material prosperity, let some
curious or courageous hand lift up but a
corner of that embroidered pall which the
superficial refinement of our privileged and
prosperous classes has thrown over society,
and how we recoil from the revelation of what
lies seething and festering beneath! How we
are startled by glimpses of hidden pain, and
covert vice, and horrible wrongs done and
suffered! Then come strange trials before
our tribunals, polluting the public mind. Then
are great blue books piled up before Parliament, filled with reports of inspectors and
committees. Then eloquent newspaper articles are let off like rockets into an abyss, just
to show the darkness, — and expire. Then
have we fitful, clamorous bursts of popular
indignation and remorse ; hasty partial remedies for antiquated mischiefs; clumsy tinker-
ing of barbarous and inadequate laws ; —

then the vain attempt to solder together undeniable truths and admitted falsehoods into
some brittle, plausible compromise ; — then at
last the slowly awakening sense of a great
want aching far down at the heart of society,
throbbing upwards and outwards with a
quicker and a quicker pulse; and then, —
what then? What if this great want, this
something which we crave and seek, be in a
manner a part of ourselves ? — lying so near
to us, so close at our feet, that we have overlooked and lost it in reaching after the distant,
the difficult, the impracticable ?

WORK in some form or other is the appointed lot of all, — divinely appointed ; and,
given as equal the religious responsibilities of
the two sexes, might we not, in distributing
the work to be done in this world, combine
and use in more equal proportion the working
faculties of men and women, and so find a
remedy for many of those mistakes which
have vitiated some of our noblest educational
and charitable institutions ? Is it not possible

that in the apportioning of the work we may have too far sundered what in God's creation never can be sundered without pain and mischief, the masculine and the feminine influences? — lost the true balance between the element of power and the element of love? and trusted too much to mere mechanical means for carrying out high religious and moral purposes?

It seems indisputable that the mutual influence of the two sexes, — brain upon brain, — life upon life, — becomes more subtle, and spiritual, and complex, more active and more intense, in proportion as the whole human race is improved and developed. The physiologist knows this well : let the moralist give heed to it, lest in becoming more intense, and active, and extended, such influences become at the same time less beneficent, less healthful, and less manageable.

It appears to me that we do wrong to legislate, and educate, and build up institutions without taking cognizance of this law of our being It appears to me that the domestic

affections and the domestic duties, — what I
have called the " communion of love and the
communion of labor," — must be taken as the
basis of all the more complicate social relations, and that the family sympathies must be
carried out and developed in all the forms and
duties of social existence, before we can have
a prosperous, healthy, happy, and truly Christian community. Yes! — I have the deepest
conviction, founded not merely on my own
experience and observation, but on the testimony of some of the wisest and best men
among us, that to enlarge the working sphere
of woman to the measure of her faculties, to
give her a more practical and authorized share
in all social arrangements which have for their
object the amelioration of evil and suffering,
is to elevate her in the social scale ; and that
whatever renders womanhood respected and
respectable in the estimation of the people
tends to humanize and refine the people.

It is surely an anomaly that, while women
are divided from men in learning and working
by certain superstitions of a conventional
morality, and in social position by the whole

spirit and tendency of our past legislation, their material existence and interests are regarded as identical; — identical, however, only in this sense, — that the material and social interests of the woman are always supposed to be merged in those of the man; while it is never taken for granted that the true interests of the man are inseparable from those of the woman; so at the outset we are met by inconsistency and confusion, such as must inevitably disturb the security and integrity of all the mutual relations.

Here, then, I take my stand, not on any hypothesis of expediency, but on what I conceive to be an essential law of life ; and I conclude that all our endowments for social good, whatever their especial purpose or denomination, — educational, sanitary, charitable, penal, — will prosper and fulfil their objects in so far as we carry out this principle of combining in due proportion the masculine and the feminine element, and will fail or become perverted into some form of evil in so far as we neglect or ignore it.

I WILL now proceed to illustrate my position by certain facts connected with the administration of various public institutions at home and abroad.

And, first, with regard to hospitals.

What is the purpose of a great hospital? Ask a physician or a surgeon, zealous in his profession : he will probably answer that a great hospital is a great medical school in which the art of healing is scientifically and experimentally taught; where the human sufferers who crowd those long vistas of beds are not men and women, but "cases" to be studied: and so under one aspect it ought to be, and must be. A great, well-ordered medical school is absolutely necessary; and to be able to regard the various aspects of disease with calm discrimination, the too sensitive human sympathies must be set aside. Therefore much need is there here of all the masculine firmness of nerve and strength of understanding. But surely a great hospital has another purpose, that for which it was originally founded and endowed, namely, as a refuge and solace for disease and suffering.

Here are congregated in terrible reality all the ills enumerated in Milton's visionary lazar-house, —

> " All maladies
> Of ghastly spasm or racking torture, qualms
> Of heart-sick agony, wide-wasting pestilence " —

I spare you the rest of the horrible catalogue. He goes on, —

> " Dire was the tossing, deep the groans; despair
> Tended the sick, busiest from couch to couch."

But why must despair tend the sick? We can imagine a far different influence " busiest from couch to couch!"

There is a passage in Tennyson's poems, written long before the days of Florence Nightingale, which proves that poets have been rightly called prophets, and see " the thing that shall be as the thing that is." I will repeat the passage. He is describing the wounded warriors nursed and tended by the learned ladies, —

> " A kindlier influence reigned, and everywhere
> Low voices with the ministering hand

> Hung round the sick. The maidens came, they talked,
> They sung, they read, till she, not fair, began
> To gather light, and she that was, became
> Her former beauty treble; to and fro,
> Like creatures native unto gracious act,
> And in their own clear element they moved."

This, you will say, is the poetical aspect of the scene; was it not poetical, too, when the poor soldier said that the very shadow of Florence Nightingale passing over his bed seemed to do him good?

But to proceed. The practical advantages, the absolute necessity of a better order of nurses to take the charge and supervision of the sick in our hospitals, is now so far admitted that it is superfluous to add anything to what I said in my former Lecture. It is not now maintained that a class of women, whom I have heard designated by those who employ them as drunken, vulgar, unfeeling, and inefficient, without any religious sense of responsibility, and hardened by the perpetual sight of suffering, are alone eligible to nurse and comfort the sick poor. One great cause of the cruelty and neglect charged against hospital nurses is, that they become insensibly and gradually hardened by perpetual sights and sounds of suffering. " A good nurse ought to receive every new case of affliction as if it were the first;" so it has been said. But if we look for this ever-fresh fount of sympathy and conscientiousness either from natural kindness of heart, sense of duty, or love of gain, we shall be disappointed. In a small hospital for wretched, helpless, bed-ridden paupers, one of the religious women acknowledged to me that their duties were of a nature so painful and revolting, and in their issue, which could end only in death, so depressing, that still, after being for years accustomed to the work, they were obliged every morning to dedicate themselves anew to their duty, "for the love of God." It is because they were *accustomed* to the work, that such a renewed and especial consecration to it in heart and soul was daily necessary: nothing hardens like custom.

" You ought to understand," said Mr. Maurice, "that the study of disease for the purpose of science has no tendency to harden the heart." True ; but to minister to disease with no ulterior purpose but self-interest, though it be of an elevated and enlightened kind, does and *must* harden the heart in the long run.

It is one cause of that languor, and despondency, and impatience, which sometimes comes over zealous and kind-hearted women who devote themselves to the sick, and miserable, and perverted, and ignorant poor, that they begin with a conviction that they shall find their reward in a certain palpable result of their labor; that after a time they shall be able to count their successes on their fingers. Those who set about fulfilling the teaching of Christ on such terms are only a degree better than those who work for hire of another kind. In what is heart-warm charity better than ambition or love of glory, if it be not in this; that those who do God's work must devote themselves to it daily in a stronger faith and in a loftier hope, in the faith that no atom of such work shall be lost or pass away?

One purpose of a hospital supposes the presence of the feminine nature to *minister*

through love as well as the masculine intellect to *rule* through power,—the presence of
those who can soothe and comfort as well as
those who can heal.   Now, I will speak of
what I have seen where this combined *regime*
prevails.

The Paris hospitals are so admirably organized by the religious women, who in almost
every instance share in the administration so
far as regards the care of the sick, that I have
often been surprised that hitherto the numbers
of our medical men who have studied at Paris
have not made any attempts to introduce a
better system of female nursing into the hospitals at home.   But they appear to have
regarded every thing of the kind with despair
or indifference.

In my former Lecture I mentioned several
of the most famous of these hospitals. During
my last visit to Paris I visited a hospital
which I had not before seen,—the hospital
Laborissiére, which appeared to me a model
of all that a civil hospital ought to be,—clean,
airy, light, and lofty, above all, cheerful.   I
should observe that generally in the hospitals

served by Sisters of Charity, there is ever an
air of cheerfulness caused by their own sweet-
ness of temper and voluntary devotion to their
work. At the time that I visited this hospital
it contained six hundred and twelve patients,
three hundred men and three hundred and
twelve women, in two ranges of building
divided by a very pretty garden. The whole
interior management is entrusted to twenty-
five trained Sisters of the same Order as those
who serve the Hôtel-Dieu. There are besides
about forty servants, men and women, — men
to do the rough work, and male nurses to
assist in the men's wards under the superintendence of the Sisters. There are three
physicians and two surgeons in constant
attendance, a steward or comptroller of accounts, and other officers. To complete this
picture, I must add that the hospital Laborissiére was founded by a lady, a rich heiress, a
married woman, too, whose husband, after her
death, carried out her intentions to the utmost
with zeal and fidelity. She had the assistance
of the best architects in France to plan her
building : medical and scientific men had

aided her with their counsels. What the feminine instinct of compassion had conceived, was by the manly intellect planned and ordered, and again by female aid administered. In all its arrangements, this hospital appeared to me a perfect example of the combined working of men and women.

In contrast with this splendid foundation, I will mention another not less admirable in its way.

When I was at Vienna, I saw a small hospital belonging to the Sisters of Charity there. The beginning had been very modest, two of the Sisters having settled in a small old house. Several of the adjoining buildings were added one after the other, connected by wooden corridors : the only new part which had any appearance of being adapted to its purpose was the infirmary, in which were fifty-two patients, twenty-six men and twenty-six women, besides nine beds for cholera. There were fifty Sisters, of whom one half were employed in the house, and the other half were going their rounds amongst the poor, or

nursing the sick in private houses. There
was a nursery for infants, whose mothers were
at work; a day-school for one hundred and
fifty girls, in which only knitting and sewing
were taught; all clean, orderly, and, above all,
cheerful. There was a dispensary, where two
of the Sisters were employed in making up
prescriptions, homœopathic and allopathic.
There was a large airy kitchen, where three
of the Sisters with two assistants were cooking. There were two priests and two physicians. So that, in fact, under this roof we
had the elements on a small scale of an
English workhouse; but very different was
the spirit which animated it.

I saw at Vienna another excellent hospital
for women alone, of which the whole administration and support rested with the ladies
of the Order of St. Elizabeth. These are
cloistered, that is, not allowed to go out of
their home to nurse the sick and poor; nor
have they any schools; but all sick women
who apply for admission are taken in without
any questions asked, so long as there is room

for them, — cases of child-birth excepted. At the time I visited this hospital it contained ninety-two patients; about twenty were cases of cholera. There were sixteen beds in each ward, over which two Sisters presided. The dispensary, which was excellently arranged, was entirely managed by two of the ladies. The Superior told me that they have always three or more Sisters preparing for their profession under the best apothecaries; and there was a large garden principally of medicinal and kitchen herbs. Nothing could exceed the purity of the air, and the cleanliness, order, and quiet everywhere apparent.

In the great civil hospital at Vienna, one of the largest I have ever seen, larger even than the Hôtel-Dieu at Paris, I found that the Sisters of Charity were about to be introduced. One of my friends there, a distinguished naturalist and philosopher as well as physician, told me that the disorderly habits and the want of intelligence in the paid female nurses, had induced him to join with his colleagues in inviting the co-operation of the religious Sisters, though it was at first rather against their will. In the hospital of St. John at Salzburg, the same change had been found necessary.

I suppose that every traveller who has visited Milan remembers at least the outside of that most venerable and beautiful building, the *'Spedale Maggiore* (the Great Hospital). The exquisite and florid grace of the façade, with its terra-cotta mouldings, suggests the idea of some fairy structure, some palace of pleasure, rather than an asylum for the sick and poor. Although I could not help feeling this want of fitness, — for fitness is the first principle of taste, — yet as an artist I was struck with admiration of the architectural elegance, and used to stand before it, entranced as by music to the eye. But it is not of the exterior, but of the interior I have now to speak. It is the largest hospital I have ever visited, larger than the Hôtel-Dieu at Paris, larger even than the great hospital at Vienna; and contained, on the day I visited it, more than twenty-five hundred patients, without reckoning those in the lying-in hospital and the hospital for foundlings and sick children, in connection with it. This large number I was told arose from a very sick season, and the prevalence of cholera: in general the number of patients does not exceed fifteen hundred. It belongs to the municipality, and is managed by six governors, each of whom is supreme acting governor for two months in the year. Forty Sisters of Charity and their Superior, with a large staff of female assistants, managed the nursing.

Had I been content, like other travellers, with admiring and studying the beautiful architecture, I should have brought away a pleasanter impression of this great hospital; but the interior disappointed me. It seemed to me *too* large, too crowded, and the management not quite satisfactory. It is the most richly endowed hospital in all Europe, and yet they say that it is deeply in debt. The change of government every two months must be injurious. I had not time to go into details, but would recommend those who are interested in such matters to study the administrative arrangements of this great hospital, and see where the good and the evil may lie. It is a great medical school.

I had, when in Piedmont, particular opportunities for learning the state of feeling in regard to the service of the hospitals, and it deserves some consideration.

A great number of the medical students were in open opposition to the Sisters employed in the hospitals, and on inquiring I found that this opposition arose from various causes. In the first place, it was generally allowed that there is a great laxity of morals, — I might give it a harder name, — prevalent among the medical students in Turin as elsewhere, and that the influence of these religious women, the strict order and surveillance exercised and enforced by them wherever they ruled, is in the highest degree distasteful to those young men; more especially the protection afforded by the Sisters to the poor young female patients, when convalescent, or after leaving the hospitals,

had actually excited a feeling against them;
though as women, and as religious women,
one might think that this was a duty, and
not the least sacred of their duties.

This adverse feeling took the color of lib-
eralism.

Now I had, and have, an intense sympathy
with the Piedmontese, in their brave struggle
for political and religious independence; but
I cannot help wishing and hoping that the
reform, in both cases, may be carried out in
the progressive, not in the destructive spirit;
and, thanks to those enlightened men who
guide the councils of Piedmont, and who do
not "mistake reverse of wrong for right," it
has hitherto been so.

It will be remembered that the Sisters of
Charity were excepted when other religious
orders were suppressed; and, in consequence,
it was a sort of fashion with an ultra party
to consider them as a part of an ecclesiastical
regime, which had been identified with all
the evils of tyranny, ignorance, and priestly
domination.   This feeling was subsiding
when I was there.   The heroism of the

sixty-two Sisters of Charity, who had accompanied the Piedmontese armies to the East, and of their Superior, Madame de Cordera, had excited in the public mind a degree of enthusiasm which silenced the vulgar and short-sighted opposition of a set of dissipated, thoughtless boys.

One thing more had occurred which struck me. A few months before my arrival, and as a part of this medical agitation, a petition or protest had been drawn up by the medical students and the young men who served in the apothecaries' shops, against the small dispensaries and infirmaries which the Sisters had of their own for the poor, and for children. The plea was, *not* that their infirmaries were ill-served or that the medicines were ill compounded, or that any mistakes had occurred from ignorance or unskilfulness, but that this small medical practice, unpaid and beneficent, " took the bread out of the men's mouths." Before we laugh at this short-sighted folly and cruelty, which supposes that the interests of the two sexes can possibly be antagonistic instead of being inseparably

bound up together, we must recollect that
we have had some specimens of the same
feeling in our own country; as for instance,
the opposition to the female school at Marlborough House, and the steady opposition
of the inferior part of the medical profession
to all female practitioners. That some departments of medicine are peculiarly suited
to women is beginning to strike the public
mind. I know that there are enlightened
and distinguished physicians both here and
in France, who take this view of the subject,
though the medical profession as a body entertain a peculiar dread of all innovation,
which they resist with as much passive per-
tinacity as boards of guardians and London
Corporations.*

* In the Memoirs of Lord Cockburn, we have an edifying
instance of the extent to which professional habits of thinking
may unconsciously verge on prejudice the most absurd and
cruel : — "In 1800, the people of Edinburgh were much
occupied about the removal of an evil in the system of their
infirmary; which evil, though strenuously defended by able
men, it is difficult now to believe could ever have existed.
The medical officers consisted at that time of the whole
members of the colleges of physicians and of surgeons, who
attended the hospital by a monthly rotation: so that the
patients had the chance of an opposite treatment, according

Before I leave Piedmont, I must mention two more hospitals, because of the contrast they afford, which will aptly illustrate the principle I am endeavoring to advocate.

The hospital of St. John at Vercelli, which I had the opportunity of inspecting minutely, left a strong impression on my mind. At the time I visited it, it contained nearly four hundred patients. There was besides, in an adjacent building, a school and hospital for poor children. The whole interior economy of these two hospitals was under the management of eighteen women, with a staff of assistants both male and female. The Superior, a very handsome, intelligent woman, had been trained at Paris, and had presided

to the whim of the doctor, every thirty days. Dr. James Gregory, whose learning extended beyond that of his profession, attacked this absurdity in one of his powerful, but wild and personal, quarto pamphlets. The public was entirely on his side, and so at last were the managers, who resolved that the medical officers should be appointed permanently, as they have ever since been. Most of the medical profession, including the whole private lecturers, and even the two colleges, who all held that the power of annoying the patients in their turn was their right, were vehement against this innovation; and some of them went to law in opposition to it."

over this provincial hospital for eleven years.
There was the same cheerfulness which I
have had occasion to remark in all institutions where the religious and feminine
elements were allowed to influence the material administration; and everything was
exquisitely clean, airy, and comfortable. In
this instance the dispensary (*Pharmacie*) was
managed by apothecaries, and not by the
women.

Now, in contrast with this hospital, I will
describe a famous hospital at Turin. It is
a recent building, with all the latest improvements, and considered, in respect to
fitness for its purpose, as a *chef-d'œuvre* of
architecture. The contrivances and material
appliances for the sick and convalescent were
exhibited to me as the wonder and boast of
the city; certainly they were most ingenious.
The management was in the hands of a
committee of gentlemen; under them a
numerous staff of priests and physicians.
Two or three female servants of the lowest
class were sweeping and cleaning. In the
convalescent wards I saw a great deal of

card-playing.   All was formal, cold, clean,
and silent; no cheerful, kindly faces, no soft
low voices, no light active figures were hov-
ering round.   I left the place with a melancholy feeling, shared as I found by those who
were with me.   One of them, an accomplished
physician, felt and candidly acknowledged the
want of female influence here.

One of the directors of the great military
hospital at Turin told me that he regarded
it as one of the best deeds of his life, that
he had recommended, and carried through,
the employment of the Sisters of Charity in
this institution.   Before the introduction of
these ladies, the sick soldiers had been nursed
by orderlies sent from the neighboring barracks, — men chosen because they were unfit
for other work.   The most rigid discipline
was necessary to keep them in order; and
the dirt, neglect, and general immorality were
frightful.   Any change was, however, resisted
by the military and medical authorities, till
the invasion of the cholera; then the orderlies
became, most of them, useless, distracted, and

almost paralyzed with terror. Some devoted Sisters of Charity were introduced in a moment of perplexity and panic; then all went well, — propriety, cleanliness, and comfort prevailed. " No day passes," said my informant, "that I do not bless God for the change which I was the humble instrument of accomplishing in this place!"

Very similar was the information I received relative to the naval hospital at Genoa; but I had not the opportunity· of visiting it.

Another excellent hospital at Turin, that of St. John, contained, when I visited it, four hundred patients, a nearly equal number of men and women. There were, besides, a separate ward for sick children, and two wards containing about sixty "incurables" — the bedridden and helpless poor, of the same class which find refuge in our workhouses. The whole of this large establishment was under the management of twenty-two religious women, with a staff of about forty-five assistants, men and women, and a large number of medical men and students. All was clean, and neat, and cheerful. I was particularly struck by the neatness with which the food was served; men brought it up in large trays, but the ladies themselves distributed it. Some friends of the poor sick were near the beds. I remember being touched by the sight of a little dog which, with its fore-paws resting on the bed and a pathetic wistful expression in its drooping face, kept its eyes steadfastly fixed on the sick man; a girl was kneeling beside him, to whom one of the Sisters was speaking words of comfort.

In this hospital and others I have found an excellent arrangement for the night-watch: it was a large sentry-box of an octagon-shape, looking each way, the upper part all of glass, but furnished with curtains; and on a kind of dresser or table were arranged writing materials, all kinds of medicine and restoratives which might be required in haste, and a supply of linen, napkins, &c. Here two Sisters watched all night long; here the accounts were kept, and the private business of the wards carried on in the daytime: a certain degree of privacy was thus secured for the ladies on duty when necessary. The

Superior, whom we should call the matron, was an elderly woman, wearing the same simple convenient religious dress as the others, and only recognized by the large bunch of keys at her girdle.

The Marchese A——, one of the governors of the *Hospice de la Maternité*, described to us in terms of horror the state in which he had found the establishment when under the management of a board of governors who employed hired matrons and nurses. At last, in despair, he sent for some trained Sisters, ten of whom, with a Superior, now directed the whole in that spirit of order, cheerfulness, and unremitting attention, which belongs to them. The Marchese particularly dwelt on their economy. " We cannot," said he, "give them unlimited means (*des fonds à discretion*), for these good ladies think that all should go to the poor; but if we allow them a fixed sum, we find they can do more with that sum than we could have believed possible, and they never go beyond it : they are admirable accountants and economists.''

I could relate much more of what I have
seen in hospitals at home and abroad; but
this Lecture is intended to be suggestive only,
and for this purpose I have said enough. Yet,
before I pass on to another part of my subject,
I must be allowed to make one or two observations on the testimony before me relative to
the moral and medical efficiency of the lady-
nurses sent to the East.

In the midst of many differences of opinion,
in one thing all are agreed. All to whom
I have spoken, without one exception, bear
witness to the salutary influence exercised by
the lady-nurses over the men, and the submission and gratitude of the patients. In the
most violent attacks of fever and delirium,
when the orderlies could not hold them down
in their beds, the mere presence of one of
these ladies, instead of being exciting, had the
effect of instantly calming the spirits and
subduing the most refractory. It is allowed
also that these ladies had the power to repress
swearing and bad and coarse language; to
prevent the smuggling of brandy and raka
into the wards; to open the hearts of the

sullen and desperate to contrition and responsive kindness. The facts are recorded, and remain uncontradicted; but the natural inference to be drawn from them does not seem to have struck our medical men.

With regard to the feeling between the nurses and the patients, here is a page of testimony which can hardly be read without emotion.

" We have attended many hundreds of the sick in the British army, suffering under every form of disease, — the weary, wasting, low typhus fever or dysentery; or the agonies of the frost bite; and they were surrounded by every accumulation of misery. For the fevered lips there was no cooling drink, for the sinking frame no strengthening food, for the wounded limb no soft pillow, for many no watchful hands to help; but never did we hear a murmur pass their lips. Those whose privilege it was to nurse them noticed only obedience to orders, respectful gratitude, patience, and the most self-denying consideration for those who ministered. Even when in an apparently dying state, they would look up in our faces and smile."

She adds in another place, with deep natural feeling, " It was so sad to see them die one after another; we learned to love them so!"

" We were trained," she says, " under the hospital nurses at home, receiving our instruction from them; and what we saw *there* of disobedience to medical orders and cruelty to patients would fill pages, and make you shudder." " More of evil language was heard in one hour in a London hospital than met my ears during months in a military one."

The drawbacks in regard to our volunteer ladies, were not want of sense nor want of zeal, but the want of robust health, experience, and sufficient training.

The experiment of a staff of the volunteer lady-nurses from St. John's House,* with paid and trained nurses under their orders, has lately been made in King's College Hospital. I think I may say that it has so far succeeded. I have the testimony of one of the gentlemen filling a high official situation at the hospital, (and who was at first opposed to the introduc-

* The training institution for nurses, in Queen Square, Westminster.

tion of these ladies, or at least most doubtful
of their success,) that they have up to this
time succeeded; that strong prejudices have
been overcome, that there has been a purifying
and harmonizing influence at work since their
arrival. The testimony borne by the ladies
themselves to the courtesy of the medical men
and the students, and the entire harmony with
which they now work together, struck me even
more.

The same conquest was obtained by the
volunteer ladies in the East. One of them
says: "So misrepresented were the army-
surgeons that the Sisters and Ladies feared
them more than any other horrors." "We
were told to expect rebuff, discouragement,
even insult. We never during this whole year
experienced any other than assistance, encouragement, gentlemanly treatment, and, from
many, the most cordial kindness." Of course
there were some exceptions, but this was to
be expected; and in reference to the principle
for which I am now pleading, "the communion of labor," I consider this testimony very
satisfactory.

I MUST now say a few words with regard to female administration in prisons.

After the revelations made by Howard seventy or eighty years ago, and their immediate effect in rousing the attention and sympathy of Europe, one would have thought it impossible to fall back into the ghastly horrors he had discovered and exposed. Yet in 1816, his name was already almost forgotten. The acts of parliament he had procured were become a dead letter, were openly and grossly violated. The very slow progress made by moral influences in the last century is very striking, taken in connection with the cold and formal scepticism which then found favor with men who fancied themselves philosophers, but were only leading a popular reaction against the formal theological superstitions of the previous century. There was, indeed, with much intellectual movement, a deadness of feeling, an indifference to the well-being of the masses, an utterly low standard of principle, religious, moral, political, which in these days of a more awakened public conscience seems hardly conceivable. We make slow work of

it now; we want a higher standard in high
places; but in this at least we are improved,
— men do not *now* dispute that such or such
things ought to be done, may be done, must
be done; unhappily they do dispute endlessly
as to the how, the when, and the where, till
they defeat their own purposes, allow great
principles to be shelved by wretched perplexities of detail, and shrink back, cowed by the
passive, stolid resistance of ignorance and
self-interest. Forty years after the publication
of Howard's " State of Prisons," what was
the state of the greatest prison in England?
When Elizabeth Fry ventured into that " den
of wild beasts," as it was called, the female
ward in Newgate, about three hundred women
were found crammed together, begging, swearing, drinking, fighting, gambling, dancing, and
dressing up in men's clothes, and two jailers
set to watch them, who stood jeering at the
door, literally afraid to enter. Elizabeth Fry
would have been as safe in the men's wards
as among her own sex; she would certainly
have exercised there an influence as healing,
as benign, as redeeming; but she did well in

the first instance, and in the *then* state of public feeling, to confine her efforts to the miserable women.*

I know that there are many persons who would receive with a laugh of scorn, or a shudder of disgust, the idea of having virtuous, religious, refined, well-educated women, brought into contact with wretched and depraved prisoners of the other sex. It would even be more revolting than the idea of a born lady, — a Florence Nightingale, or a Miss Anderson, or a Miss Shaw Stewart, — nursing a wounded soldier, appeared only two years ago. Yet this is precisely what I wish to see tried. Captain Maconochie mentions the influence which his wife exercised over the most hardened and horrible criminals, the convicts at Norfolk Island: because she was fearless,

* The act of parliament procured through Mrs. Fry's influence, ordered the appointment of matrons and female officers in all our prisons; but no provision has been made for their proper training, nor are the qualifications at all defined.

My idea is that, besides a superior order of female superintendents, we should have lady visitors also, as it is like an infusion of fresh life and energy; but I do not think that such visiting should be confined to the female wards.

and gentle, and a *woman*, those men respected
her, — they who respected nothing else in
heaven or earth. It was something like the
sanitary influence which the surgeon's wife
exercised over the cholera patients in a military hospital, and which I mentioned in my
former Lecture.* Such instances might be
multiplied ; — indeed many such cases are
matters of notoriety ; but so far as I can see,
they are always regarded as the consequence
of accident, not the result of an essential law ;
they have led to no farther experiments, and
no inference to guide us systematically has
been drawn from them.

In my Lecture last year I mentioned the
employment of trained Sisters of Charity in
some of the prisons of Piedmont. When I
was there a few months ago, I obtained, by
the courtesy of our ambassador, a written
memorandum of the rules and regulations
applied to them, the conditions under which
they were employed, and the price paid for
their services to the religious institutions they

* Vide " Sisters of Charity," p. 126.

belonged to. I think it unnecessary to give here the twenty-three articles of this regulation, which would not be applicable, at least only partially applicable, in this country. It appears that twenty-eight of these ladies are employed in five reformatory prisons (one of which is for females, the others for men), and that eight of the other prisons (*Carceri giudiziarie*) are partly administered by the " *Suore,*" but the number was not fixed in each prison.

In the general Report on the condition of the prisons, addressed to the Minister of the Interior, I found this paragraph, which I translate from the original Italian, —

" It is an indisputable fact that the prisons which are served by the Sisters are the best ordered, the most cleanly, and in all respects the best regulated in the country; hence it is to be desired that the number should be increased; and this is the more desirable, because where the Sisters are not established the criminal women are under the charge of jailers of the other sex, which ought not to be tolerated."

To this I add the testimony of the Minister

himself from a private communication : "Not
only have we experienced the advantage
of employing the Sisters of Charity in the
prisons, in the supervision of the details, in
distributing food, preparing medicines, and
nursing the sick in the infirmaries; but we
find that the influence of these ladies on the
minds of the prisoners, when recovering from
sickness, has been productive of the greatest
benefit, as leading to permanent reform in
many cases, and a better frame of mind always ; for this reason, among others, we have
given them every encouragement." *

Among the other reasons alluded to, the
greater economy of the management was a
principal one. It is admitted, even by those
who are opposed to them, that in the administration of details these women can always
make a given sum go farther than the paid
officials of the other sex. I must add that, in
some of the prisons mentioned to me, canteens

* In my former Lecture ("Sisters of Charity,") I alluded
to the employment of women in the prisons of Piedmont.
My visit to Turin in November, 1855, confirmed by personal
knowledge and inquiry the testimony already received on this
point.

were allowed, where the prisoners, besides their rations, might purchase various indulgences. These canteens were placed under the direction of the Sisters ; but as they protested against the sale of wine and brandy to the prisoners, except when medically prescribed, some disagreement arose between them and the other officials, and I do not know how it terminated.

Even at the risk of wearying you with this part of my subject, I will venture to describe, as briefly as I can, a certain reformatory prison of a very unusual kind, and which left a strong impression on my mind of the good that may be effected by very simple means. A prison governed chiefly by women, — and the women as well as the men who directed it responsible only to the Government, and not merely subordinate like the female officers in our prisons, — was a singular spectacle ; and I hope it will be distinctly understood that in describing what I have seen, it is not with any idea that these arrangements could be or

ought to be, *exactly* imitated among us. I
only suggest the facts as illustrative of the
principle I advocate, and as worthy of the
consideration of humane and philosophic
thinkers.

This prison at Neudorf is an experiment
which as yet has only had a three years' trial,
but it has so completely succeeded up to this
time that they are preparing to organize eleven
other prisons on the same plan.   From a
conversation I had with one of the Government officers, I could understand that the
economy of the administration is a strong
recommendation, as well as the moral success.
Its origin is worth mentioning.   It began by
the efforts made by two humane ladies to find
a refuge for those wretched creatures of their
own sex who, after undergoing their term of
punishment, were cast out of the prisons.
These ladies, not finding at hand any persons
prepared to carry out their views, sent to
France for two women of a religious order
which was founded for the reformation of lost
and depraved women ; and two of the Sisters
were sent from Angers accordingly.   After a

while this small institution attracted the notice of the . Government. It was taken in hand officially, enlarged, and organized as a prison as well as a penitentiary; the original plan being strictly adhered to, and the same management retained.

At the time that I visited it, this prison consisted of several different buildings, and a large garden enclosed by high walls. The inmates were divided into three classes, completely separated. The first were the criminals, the most desperate characters, brought there from the prisons at Vienna, and the very refuse of those prisons. They had been brought there six or eight at a time, fettered hand and foot, and guarded by soldiers and policemen.

The second class, drafted from the first, were called the penitents; they were allowed to assist in the house, to cook, and to wash, and to work in the garden, which last was a great boon. There were more than fifty of this class.

The third class were the voluntaries, those who, when their term of punishment and penitence had expired, preferred remaining in the house, and were allowed to do so. They were employed in a work of which a part of the profit was retained for their benefit. There were about twelve or fourteen of this class. The whole number of criminals then in the prison exceeded two hundred, and they expected more the next day.

To manage these unhappy, disordered, perverted creatures, there were twelve women, assisted by three chaplains, a surgeon, and a physician: none of the men resided in the house, but visited it every day. The soldiers and police officers, who had been sent in the first instance as guards and jailers, had been dismissed. The dignity, good sense, patience, and tenderness of this female board of management were extraordinary. The ventilation and the cleanliness were perfect; while the food, beds, and furniture were of the very coarsest kind. The medical supervision was important, where there was as much disease, — of frightful, physical disease, — as there was of moral disease, crime, and misery. There was a surgeon and physician, who visited daily. There was a dispensary, under the care of two Sisters, who acted as chief nurses and apothecaries. One of these was busy with the sick, the other went round with me. She was a little, active woman, not more than two or three and thirty, with a most cheerful face and bright, kind, dark eyes. She had been two years in the prison, and had previously received a careful training of five years, — three years in the general duties of her vocation, and two years of medical training. She spoke with great intelligence of the differences of individual temperament, requiring a different medical and moral treatment.

The Sister who superintended the care of the criminals was the oldest I saw, and she was bright-looking also. The Superior, who presided over the whole establishment, had a serious look, and a pale, care-worn, but perfectly mild and dignified face.

The differences between the countenances of those criminals who had lately arrived, and those who had been admitted into the class of penitents, was extraordinary. The first were either stupid, gross, and vacant, or absolutely frightful from the predominance of evil propensities. The latter were at least humanized.

When I expressed my astonishment that so small a number of women could manage such a set of wild and wicked creatures, the answer was: "If we want assistance we shall have it; but it is as easy with our system to manage two hundred or three hundred as one hundred or fifty." She then added devoutly, "The power is not in ourselves; it is granted from above." It was plain that she had the most perfect faith in that power, and in the text which declared all things possible to faith.

We must bear in mind that here men and women were acting together; that in all the regulations, religious and sanitary, there was mutual aid, mutual respect, an interchange of experience; but the women were subordinate only to the chief civil and ecclessiastical authority; the internal administration rested with them.*

* I hope it will be remembered here, and in other parts of this essay, that I am not arguing for any particular system

If what I have said of the salutary effects of female influence in prisons carry any weight, yet more does it apply to the employment of superior women in the Reformatory schools for young criminals. Profligate boys, accustomed to see only the most coarse and depraved women (their own female relatives are in general examples of the worst class), would be especially touched and tamed by the mere presence of a better order of women. I observe that in the last report of the school at Mettrai, mention is made of the nine Sisters of Charity who are employed to superintend the kitchen and infirmary; which last consists of a ward with about ten beds, and a corridor where the Sisters receive the out-patients; and to the constant watchfulness, medical skill, and gentle influence of these women much good is attributed.

Mr. Hill, in his work on Crime, in speaking of the officials in the reformatory prisons for

of administration, or discipline, or kind or degree of punishment; but merely for this principle, that whatever the system selected as the best, it should be carried out by a due admixture of female influence and management combined with the man's government.

boys, says expressly that some of these officials
ought to be women " for the sake of female
influence, and to call into action those family
feelings, which Mr. Sidney Turner and Miss
Carpenter think of such vital importance in
the process of reformation." This is precisely
the principle for which I am pleading, and in
organizing the new reformatory institutions it
might be advantageously kept in view.

" It should be remembered," adds Mr. Hill,
" that up to the time of his commitment, a
criminal has often had no one to give him
counsel or sympathy, no virtuous parent or
kind relative to feel for him or guide him
aright, and that there is consequently in his
case a void which is perhaps first filled up by a
kind prison officer. This may account for the
almost filial affection often shown, particularly
by the younger prisoners, towards a good governor, chaplain, or matron." What we have
now to do is to enlarge the application of this
principle.

The extreme difficulty of finding masters at
the best of all our reformatory schools, that at

Redhill, was the subject discussed in a recent
meeting of benevolent and intelligent men,
interested in this institution. I happened to
be present. I heard the qualifications for a
master to be set over these unhappy little
delinquents thus described : — He must have
great tenderness and kindness of heart, great
power of calling forth and sympathizing with
the least manifestations of goodness or hope-
fulness; quick perception of character; great
firmness, and judgment, and command of
temper; skill in some handicraft, as carpenter-
ing and gardening; a dignified, or at least
attractive, presence, and good manners, — the
personal qualities and appearance being found
of consequence to impress the boys with respect. Now it is just possible that all these
rare and admirable qualities, some of which
God has given in a larger degree to the
woman and others to the man, might be
found combined in one man ; but such a man
has not yet been met with, and many such
would hardly be found for a stipend of 30*l.* or
40*l.* a year. Then, in this dilemma, instead
of insisting on a combination of the *paternal*

and the *maternal* qualifications in one person, might it not be possible, by associating some well educated and well trained women in the administration of these schools, to produce the required influences, — the tenderness, the sympathy, the superior manners, and refined deportment on one hand, and the firmness and energy, the manly government, and skill in handicrafts and gardening, on the other? This solution was not proposed by any one of the gentlemen who spoke; it did not seem to occur to any one present; and yet is it not worth consideration? At all events I must express my conviction that, going on as they are now doing, without the combination of those influences which ought to represent in such a community the maternal and sisterly, as well as the paternal and fraternal, relations of the home, their efforts will be in vain; their admirable institution will fall to pieces sooner or later, and people will attribute such a result to every possible cause except the real one.

The reformatory schools for perverted and

criminal girls present many more difficulties than those for boys. I do not know how it is intended to meet these especial difficulties, nor what consideration has as yet been given to them, nor in whose hands the administration of these reformatory schools is to be placed; for all I have as yet heard upon the subject, and all the pamphlets and authorities I have been able to consult, have reference principally to the treatment of delinquent boys, and very little mention is made of the poor female children of the " perishing and dangerous class " — (*perishing* and *dangerous* in every sense of these words they too surely are!) One thing is most certain, that in their case the supervision of pure-minded, humane, intelligent, and experienced men will be as necessary as the feminine element in the reformatory schools for boys; and for similar reasons, medical knowledge will be required in addition to the moral and religious influences. This has, I think, obtained too little consideration, and it is one of great importance

It is worth noticing that a proposal, made during this last session of parliament,* to aid the female penitentiaries by a grant of public money, however small, and thus obtain from the government the mere recognition of the existence of such institutions and their necessity, fell to the ground; even the usual deprecatory intimation that it would be "considered and brought forward next session," — the common device by which troublesome propositions are stifled or shuffled off, — was not here vouchsafed : the motion was received with absolute silence, and set aside by a few words from the speaker.

I can conceive that there might be many reasons for this reluctance to discuss such themes officially. It might not only offend the nice decorum of our House of Commons; it might perhaps awaken in some generous and conscientious minds a keener touch of retrospective pity, a more acute and self-reproachful pain. Let us, therefore, set the past aside; let us accept the excuse that a far lower standard of feeling and opinion

* July 15, 1856.

existed on this miserable subject some years ago; and let us think with gratitude of the more hopeful present, of the wiser and better future which we may anticipate both for men and women.

And since these female reformatories must eventually find their place among the public exigencies to be considered, one may ask, what makes the case of poor, depraved, delinquent girls far worse in itself, far more difficult to deal with, far more hopeless altogether, than that of depraved delinquent boys? How is it, that, below the lowest class of men, there is a lower class of women, abashed by the total loss of self-respect, and perverse from a sense of perpetual wrong? It is so, we are told; but why is it so? Does it arise from the greater delicacy of the organization, — from the perpetual outrage to the *nature* of the creature thus sacrificed? I cannot go into these questions at present. I must leave them to be considered and settled by such of our medical men and our clergy who may be, — what all of them ought to be, — what our Saviour was on earth, — mor-

alists and philosophers; for these questions
are of the deepest import, and must be settled sooner or later.   Meantime it is allowed
that the female reformatories now existing
are utterly insignificant ·and inadequate in
comparison to the existing amount of evil
and misery; it is allowed that they present
peculiar and unmanageable difficulties, that
they are not successful, even the best of them.
You hear it said that a hundredfold of the
money, the labor, expended on them ought
not to be regarded as thrown away, if but
one soul out of twenty were redeemed from
perdition.   All very proper and very pious.
But how is it that in this case nineteen souls
out of the twenty are supposed to be con-
signed to a perdition past cure, past hope,
past help?   The truth is, that it is not merely
the peculiar difficulties, nor the horror of corrupting influences, which interpose to prevent
success : it is the incredible rashness and
almost incredible mistakes of those who ig-
norantly, but in perfect good faith and self-
complacency, undertake a task which requires
all the aid of long training, experience, and

knowledge, combined with the impulses of benevolence, the support of religious faith, — and, I will add, a genuine vocation such as I have seen in some characters.

When I was at Turin, I visited an institution for the redemption of "unfortunate girls," (as they call themselves,* poor creatures!) which appeared to me peculiarly successful. I did not consider it perfect, nor could all its details be imitated here. Yet some of the *natural* principles, recognized and carried out, appeared to me most important. It seemed to have achieved for female victims and delinquents what Mettrai has done for those of the other sex.

This institution (called at Turin *il Refugio*, the Refuge) was founded nearly thirty years ago by a "good Christian," whose name was not given to me, but who still lives, a very old man. When his means were exhausted he had recourse to the Marquise de Barol,

---

* If you ask a good-looking girl in a hospital, or the infirmary of a workhouse, what is her condition of life, she will perhaps answer, "If you please, ma'am, I'm an unfortunate girl," in a tone of languid indifference, as if it were a profession like any other.

who has from that time devoted her life, and the greater part of her possessions, to the objects of this institution.

In the Memoirs of Mrs. Fry* there may be found a letter which Madame de Barol addressed to her on the subject of this institution and its objects, when it had existed for three or four years only. The letter is dated 1829, and is very interesting. Madame de Barol told me candidly, in 1855, that in the commencement she had made mistakes: she had been too severe. It had required twenty years of reflection, experience, and the most able assistance, to work out her purposes.

The institution began on a small scale with few inmates: it now covers a large space of ground, and several ranges of buildings for various departments, all connected, and yet most carefully separated. There are several distinct gardens enclosed by these buildings, and the green trees and flowers give an appearance of cheerfulness to the whole.

There is, first, a refuge for casual and extreme wretchedness. A certificate from a

* Vol. ii. p. 39.

priest or a physician is required, but often dispensed with. I saw a child brought into this place by its weeping and despairing mother, — a child about ten years old and in a fearful state. There was no certificate in this case, but the wretched little creature was taken in at once. There is an infirmary admirably managed by a good physician and two medical Sisters of a religious order. There are also convalescent wards. These parts of the building are kept separate, and the inmates carefully classed, all the younger patients being in a separate ward.

In the penitentiary and schools, forming the second department, the young girls and children are kept distinct from the elder ones, and those who had lately entered from the others. I saw about twenty girls under the age of fifteen, but only a few together in one room. Only a few were tolerably handsome; many looked intelligent and kindly. In one of these rooms I found a tame thrush hopping about, and I remember a girl with a soft face crumbling some bread for it, saved from her dinner. Reading, writing, plain work, and embroidery are taught, also cooking, and other domestic work. A certain number assisted by rotation in the large, lightsome kitchens and the general service of the house, but not till they had been there some months, and had received badges for good conduct. There are three gradations of these badges of merit, earned by various terms of probation. It was quite clear to me that these badges were worn with pleasure: whenever I fixed my eyes upon the little bits of red or blue ribbon, attached to the dress, and smiled approbation, I was met by a responsive smile, — sometimes by a deep, modest blush. The third and highest order of merit, which was a certificate of good conduct and steady industry during three years at least, conferred the privilege of entering an order destined to nurse the sick in the infirmary, or entrusted to keep order in the small classes. They had also a still higher privilege. And now I come to a part of the institution which excited my strongest sympathy and admiration. Appended to it is an infant hospital for the children of the very lowest orders, — children born diseased or deformed, or maimed by accidents, — epileptic, or crippled. In this hospital were thirty-two poor suffering infants, carefully tended by such of the penitents as had earned this privilege. On a rainy day I found these poor little things taking their daily exercise in a long airy corridor. Over the clean shining floor was spread temporarily a piece of coarse grey drugget, that their feet might not slip; and so they were led along, creeping, crawling, or trying to walk or run, with bandaged heads and limbs, — carefully and tenderly helped and watched by the nurses, who were themselves under the supervision of one of the religious Sisters already mentioned.

There is a good dispensary, well supplied with common medicines, and served by a well instructed Sister of Charity, with the help of one of the inmates whom she had trained.

Any inmate is free to leave the Refuge whenever she pleases, and may be received a second time, but not a third time.

I was told that when these girls leave the institution, after a probation of three or four

years, there is no difficulty in finding them
good places, as servants, cooks, washerwomen,
and even nurses; but all do not leave it.
Those who, after a residence of six years,
preferred to remain, might do so: they were
devoted to a religious and laborious life, and
lived in a part of the building which had a
sort of conventual sanctity and seclusion.
They are styled "*les Magdeleines*" (Magda-
lens). I saw sixteen of such; and I had the
opportunity of observing them. They were
all superior in countenance and organization,
and belonged apparently to a better class.
They were averse to re-entering the world,
had been disgusted and humiliated by their
bitter experience of vice, and disliked or were
unfitted for servile occupations. They had a
manufactory of artificial flowers, were skilful
embroiderers and needlewomen, and supported themselves by the produce of their work.
They were no longer objects of pity or dependent on charity; they had become objects
of respect, — and more than respect, of reverence. One of them, who had a talent for
music, Madame de Barol had caused to be

properly instructed: she was the organist of
the chapel, and the music mistress; she had
taught several of her companions to sing.
A piano stood in the centre of the room, and
they executed a little concert for us; every
thing was done easily and quietly, without
effort or display. When I looked in the faces
of these young women, — the eldest was not
more than thirty, — so serene, so healthful,
and in some instances so dignified, I found
it difficult to recall the depth of misery, degradation, and disease out of which they had
risen.

The whole number of inmates was about
one hundred and forty, without reckoning the
thirty-two sick children. Madame de Barol
said that this infant hospital was a most
efficient means of thorough reform; it called
out what was best in the disposition of the
penitents, and was indeed a test of the character and temper.*

* The above account of the Penitentiary at Turin, is from
memoranda made on the spot, and from verbal information in
November, 1855.

I have since received (while this sheet is going through the
press) a letter from a very accomplished and benevolent eccle-

If this institution had been more in the country, and if some of the penitents (or patients), whose robust *physique* seemed to require it, could have been provided with plenty of work in the open air, such as gardening, keeping cows or poultry, &c., I should have considered the arrangements, for a Catholic country, perfect. They are calculated to fulfil all the conditions of moral and physical convalescence; early rising; regular, active, *useful* employment; thorough cleanliness; the strictest order; an even, rather cool temperature; abundance of light and fresh air; and more than these, religious hope wisely and

siastic, containing some farther particulars relative to Madame de Barol's Institution. It appears that the number of inmates is at present two hundred.

The Refuge itself, and the ground on which it stands, were purchased by the government, after Madame de Barol had expended a large sum of money in the original arrangements. The government granted 10,000 fr. a year to the necessary expenses, and have since made over the Penitentiary to the Commonalty of Turin; but the hospital for the children, and the convent with the gardens adjoining, have been erected on land belonging to Madame de Barol, and at her sole expense. The infant hospital contains eighty beds. The whole institution is managed by Madame de Barol, and she has the entire control of the funds which the city has placed at her disposal, in addition to those contributed by herself.

kindly cultivated; companionship, cheerfulness, and the opportunity of exercising the
sympathetic and benevolent affections.

If these conditions could be adopted in
some of the female penitentiaries at home, I
think failure would be less common; but
since the difficulty of redemption is found to
be so great, should we not take the more
thought for prevention? Among the causes
of the evil are some which I should not like to
touch upon here; but there are others, and
not the least important, which may be discussed without offence. The small payment
and the limited sphere of employment allotted
to the women of the working classes are mentioned, by a competent witness, as one of the
causes of vice leading to crime. " Much I
believe would be done towards securing the
virtue of the female sex, and therefore towards
the general diminution of profligacy, if the
practical injustice were put an end to by
which women are excluded from many kinds
of employment for which they are naturally
qualified. The general monopoly which the
members of the stronger sex have established

for themselves is surely most unjust, and, like all other kinds of injustice, recoils on its perpetrators." * The same writer observes in another place: — " The payment for the labor of females in this country is often so small as to demand, for obtaining an honest living, a greater power of endurance and self-control than can reasonably be expected."

Here, then, is the direct testimony of an experienced man, that the more we can employ women in work fitted to their powers, the stronger the barrier we shall oppose to misery and intemperance, and more especially to that pestilence " which walketh in darkness," and to which we can hardly bring ourselves to give a name.

————

I COME now to an institution peculiar to ourselves; and truly can I affirm that if ever the combination of female with masculine supervision were imperatively needed, it is in an English parish workhouse. Really it is not

* On Crime, its Amount, Causes, and Remedies, by F. Hill, p. 85.

without a mingled feeling of shame and fear
that I approach the subject. I shall be told
that it is very un-English and very unpatriotic
to expose our social delinquencies, — particularly as I have just been praising some foreign
institutions. It is not an excuse for us that
on some points other nations are as bad as
ourselves, or worse; but it is a disgrace to us
if they are in advance on those very points
where publicity and freedom of discussion
ought to have shielded us from mistake.

I have seen many workhouses, and of all
grades. The regulation of details varies in
different parishes. Some are admirably clean,
and, as far as mere machinery can go, admirably managed; some are dirty and ill ven-
tilated; and one or two, as we learn from
recent disclosures, quite in a disgraceful state:
but whatever the arrangement and condition,
in one thing I found all alike; — the want of a
proper moral supervision. I do not say this in
the grossest sense; though even in *that* sense,
I have known of things I could hardly speak
of. But surely I may say there is want of
proper *moral* supervision where the most vul-

gar of human beings arc set to rule over the
most vulgar; where the pauper is set to manage the pauper; where the ignorant govern
the ignorant; where the aged and infirm minister to the aged and infirm; where every
softening and elevating influence is absent, or
of rare occurrence, and every hardening and
depraving influence continuous and ever at
hand. Never did I visit any dungeon, any
abode of crime or misery, in any country,
which left the same crushing sense of sorrow,
indignation, and compassion, — almost despair, — as some of our English workhouses.
Never did I see more clearly what must be the
inevitable consequences, where the feminine
and religious influences are ignored; where
what we call charity is worked by a stern,
hard machinery; where what we mean for
good is not bestowed but inflicted on others,
in a spirit not pitiful nor merciful, but reluc-
tant and adverse, if not cruel. Perhaps those
who hear me may not all be aware of the
origin of our parish workhouses. They were
intended to be religious and charitable institutions, to supply the place of those conventual

hospitals and charities which, with their reve-
nues, were suppressed by Henry VIII. For
our Reformation I am thankful, as those
should be to whom liberty of thought is dear;
but I cannot help wishing, with Dr. Arnold,
that in our country it had been carried out by
purer minds and cleaner hands; that "the
badness of the agents had not disgraced the
goodness of the cause;" that in rooting up
evils and abuses, long rooted charities had not
also been torn up. I cannot say that as yet
our parish workhouses have replaced them, in
this sense. The epithet *charitable* could never
be applied to any parish workhouse I have
seen. Our machine charity is as much *charity*,
in the Christian sense, as the praying machines
of the Tartars are piety.

The purpose of a workhouse is to be a
refuge to the homeless, houseless, helpless
poor; to night-wanderers; to orphan children
to the lame and blind; to the aged, who here
lie down on their last bed to die.

The number of inmates varies in different
parishes at different seasons, from four hun-

dred to one thousand. In the great London unions it is generally from fifteen hundred to two thousand.

These institutions are supported by a variable tax, paid so reluctantly, with so little sympathy in its purpose, that the wretched paupers seem to be regarded as a sort of parish locusts sent to devour the substance of the rate-payers, — as the natural enemies of those who are taxed for their subsistence, — almost as criminals; and I have no hesitation in saying that the convicts in some of our jails have more charitable and more respectful treatment than the poor in our workhouses: hence a notion prevails among the working classes that it is better to be a criminal than a pauper; better to go to a jail than a workhouse; and to all appearance it is so.

The administration of the parish funds for the purposes of charity is in the hands of a board of parish officers, who are *elected*, — but I do not know on what principle of *selection*, — to discharge one of the most sacred trusts that can be exercised by any responsible human being.

Between the poor and their so-called "guardians," the bond is anything but charity. I have known men among them conscientious and kindly, and willing to give time and trouble; but in a board of guardians, the *gentlemen*, that is, the well educated, intelligent, and compassionate, are generally in a minority, and can do little or nothing against the passive resistance to all innovation, the most obdurate prejudices, the most vulgar jealousy. A gentleman who had served the office said to me, "I am really unfit to be a poor-law guardian; I have some vestige of humanity left in me!"

Under these guardians are the officials, who are brought into immediate contact with the poor; a master and a matron, who keep the accounts, distribute food and clothing, and keep order. Among them, some are respected and loved, others hated or feared; some are kindly and intelligent, others of the lowest grade. What were the antecedents of these officials, what the qualifications required, and upon whom rested the deep responsibility of the choice, I never clearly understood. In

one workhouse the master had been a policeman; in another, the keeper of a small public-
house; in another, he had served in the same
workhouse as porter. Where the duties are
merely mechanical, and nothing required but
to work the material machinery of a stringent
system, this may answer very well. The
subordinates are not of a higher grade, except
occasionally the schoolmasters and school-
mistresses, whom I have sometimes found
struggling to perform their duties, sometimes
quite unfitted for them, and sometimes re-
signed to routine and despair.

In the wards for the old and the sick, the
intense vulgarity, the melancholy dulness,
mingled with a strange license and levity, are
dreadful. I attribute both the dulness and
the levity to the total absence of the religious
and the feminine element.

But you will say, how can the religious
element be wanting? Is there not always a
chaplain? The chaplain has seemed to me,
in such places, rather a religious accident,
than a religious element; when most good
and zealous, his can be no constant and per-

vading influence. When he visits a ward to
read and pray once a week, perhaps there is
decorum in his presence; the oaths, the curses,
the vile language cease, the vulgar strife is silenced,—to recommence the moment his back
is turned. I know one instance in which the
chaplain had been ill for two months, and no
one had supplied his place, except for the
Sunday services, where the bed-ridden poor
cannot attend. I remember an instance in
which the chaplain had requested that the
poor profligate women might be kept out of
his way:—they had, indeed, shown themselves somewhat obstreperous and irreverent.*
I saw, not long ago, a chaplain of a great
workhouse so dirty and shabby, that I should
have mistaken him for one of the paupers.
In doing his duty he would fling a surplice
over his dirty, torn coat, kneel down at the
entrance of a ward, not even giving himself

* Perhaps he was not so much to blame. "Over the
younger women in workhouses authority is powerless; they
will not listen to the clergymen, even could he specially address himself to them. I do not know how these are to be
reached by any existing means." Such is the testimony of
an exemplary clergyman, a chaplain in a workhouse.

the trouble to advance to the middle of the room, hurry over two or three prayers, heard from the few beds nearest to him, and then, off to another ward. The salary of this priest for the sick and the poor was twenty pounds a year. This, then, is the religious element; — as if religion were not the necessary, inseparable, ever-present, informing spirit of a Christian charitable institution, but rather something extraneous and occasional, to be taken in set doses at set times. To awaken the faith, to rouse the conscience, to heal the broken in spirit, to light up the stupefied faculties of a thousand unhappy, ignorant, debased human beings congregated together, — can a chaplain going his weekly rounds suffice for this?

Then, as to the feminine element, I will describe it. In a great and well ordered workhouse, under conscientious management, I visited sixteen wards, in each ward from fifteen to twenty-five sick, aged, bed-ridden, or, as in some cases, idle and helpless poor. In each ward all the assistance given and all the supervision were in the hands of one nurse and a "helper," both chosen from among the pauper women who were supposed to be the least immoral and drunken. The ages of the nurses might be from sixty-five to eighty; the assistants were younger.* I recollect seeing, in a provincial workhouse, a ward in which were ten old women, all helpless and bed-ridden: to nurse them was a decrepit old woman of seventy, lean, and withered, and feeble;† and her assistant was a girl with one eye, and scarcely able to see with the other. In a ward where I found eight paralyzed old women, the nurse being equally aged, the helper was a girl who had lost the use of one hand. Only the other day, I saw a pauper nurse in a sick ward who had a wooden leg. I remember no cheerful faces: when the fea-

* "The number of inmates under medical treatment in the year 1854 in the London workhouses, was over fifty thousand, omitting one workhouse (the Marylebone). There are seventy paid nurses, and five hundred pauper nurses and assistants. One half of these nurses are above fifty, one quarter above sixty, many not less than seventy, and some more than eighty years old."

† As the unpaid pauper nurses have some little additional allowance of tea or beer, it is not unusual for the medical attendant to send such poor, feeble, old women as require some little indulgence to be nurses in the sick wards.

tures and deportment were not debased by
drunkenness, or stupidity, or ill-humor, they
were melancholy, or sullen, or bloated, or
harsh : — and these are the Sisters of Charity
to whom our sick poor are confided!

In one workhouse the nurses had a penny
a week and extra beer; in another the allowance had been a shilling a month, but
recently withdrawn by the guardians from
motives of economy. The matron told me
that while this allowance continued, she could
exercise a certain power over the nurses, —
she could stop their allowance if they did
not behave well; now she has no hold on
them! In another workhouse, I asked the
matron to point out one whom she considered the best conducted and most efficient
nurse. She pointed to a crabbed, energetic-
looking old woman: "*She* is active, and
cleanly, and to be depended on so long as we
can keep her from drink. But they all drink!
Whenever it is their turn to go out for a
few hours they come back intoxicated, and
have to be put to bed:" — put to bed intox
icated in the wards they are set to rule over!

The patients often hate the nurses, and have not fear or respect enough to prevent them from returning their bad language and abuse. Of the sort of attention paid to helpless creatures under their care you may perhaps form some idea. I know that in one workhouse a poor woman could get no help but by bribery; any little extra allowance of tea or sugar left by pitying friends went in this manner. The friends and relations, themselves poor, who came to visit some bed-ridden parent, or maimed husband, or idiotic child, generally brought some trifle to bribe the nurses; and I have heard of a nurse who made five shillings a week by thus fleecing the poor inmates and their friends in pennies and sixpences. Those who would not pay this tax were neglected, and implored in vain to be turned in their beds. The matron knows that these things exist, but she has no power to prevent them; she exercises no *moral* authority; she sees that the beds are clean, the floor daily scoured, the food duly distributed; what tyranny may be exercised in her absence by these old hags,

her deputies, she has no means of knowing;
for the wretched creatures dare not complain,
knowing how it would be visited upon them.
I will not now torture you by a description
of what I know to have been inflicted and
endured in these abodes of pauperism, —
the perpetual scolding, squabbling, swearing.
Neither peace, nor forbearance, nor mutual
respect is there, nor reverence, nor gratitude.
What perhaps has shocked me most was to
discover, in the corner of one of these wards,
a poor creature who had seen better days;
to be startled when I went up to speak
to one whose features or countenance had
attracted me, by being answered in the
unmistakeable tone and language of the
well-bred and the well-born; and this has
happened to me, not once, but several times.
I never can understand why some discrimination should not be shown, unless it be
that not one of those employed is of a
grade, mental or moral, to be entrusted with
such a power of discrimination.   It is thought
that no distinction ought to be made, where
the necessary condition of entrance — poverty

— is common to all; that no more regard
should be had in the workhouse to the causes
and antecedents of poverty than in a prison
to the causes and antecedents of crime. Then
there is the rule, that this refuge for the poor
man is to be made as distasteful to the poor
man as possible. But cannot some means
be used to exclude the undeserving? Why
should this last home of the poor be not only
distasteful but deteriorating?

In some workhouses many who can work
will not, and there is no power to compel
them. In others, the inmates are confined
to such labor as is degrading and disgraceful,
— the sort of labor which is a punishment
in prisons, — which excites no faculty of attention, or hope, or sympathy, — which con-
templates neither utility nor improvement, —
such as picking oakum, &c.; and this lest
there should exist some kind of competition
injurious to tradesmen. Now this is surely
a cruel and short-sighted policy, equally unjust and injurious.*

* See Dixon's Life of Howard for an account of the changes
introduced by Joseph II. into the *Maison de Force* at Ghent.

Besides the sick and the miserable, there are also to be found the vicious, the reckless, the utterly depraved; and I could not discover that there is any system of gentle religious discipline which aimed at the reforming of the bad, or the separation of the bad from the good, except in one of our great metropolitan workhouses. The depraved women bring contamination with them; the unwed mothers, who come to lie-in, go out laughing, with a promise to come again; and they do come again and again for the same purpose. The loudest tongues, the most violent tempers, the *she-bullies* as they are called, always are the best off; the gentler spirit sinks down, lies still, perhaps for six, or eight, or twelve years, — I have seen such, — and so waits for death.

When it was said that in a certain work-

All work was discontinued which could interfere with the interests of the manufacturers. Idleness introduced disease and vice. The rooms were to be less clean and comfortable. The sojourn was to be made as disagreeable as possible. The result was found to be dreadfully demoralizing to the inmates, and not serviceable to those whom it was intended to protect.

house the out-door relief bestowed had been distributed to creatures penned up for hours in foul air, who had waited for the bread doled out with curses, and received with sullen unthankfulness, as if they had been dogs; the answer was, that many of these unhappy beings had become, from their perverted instincts, their fierce natures, and base insolence, and servile cunning, little better than brutes; and that " it was complimenting them too highly to compare them to dogs." But what has made them so? It is the system of which I complain, which brings a vulgar and a brutal power to bear on vulgarity and brutality, the bad and defective organization to bear on one bad and defective; so you increase, and multiply, and excite as in a hot-bed all the material of evil, instead of neutralizing it with good; and thus leavened you turn it out on society to contaminate all around.* What has

---

* That I may not be accused of exaggeration, I refer to the excellent lecture of the Rev. J. S. Brewer, for many years a workhouse chaplain. — See *Lectures to Ladies on Practical Subjects*, p. 271.

ground humanity out of them, but a system which ignores the force of the natural and domestic relations, and trusts to no influence but a mere machinery? A keeper of a prison once relating how his wife had at last reformed a notorious drunkard, who had been many times in prison, and was considered incorrigible, — " Ma'am," said he, " she *mithered* him so that he could not help reforming; he got to dread her sair face more than a policeman or a sheriff." This reminds me of the speech of the poor wounded soldier to one of the lady nurses at Kulali: " You are as good to me as a mother," said he, looking up in her face, " and better than a mother for all that I know!" A great, tall, working man was pouring out some domestic story to a friend of mine, when, stopping short, he said, " I beg your pardon, ma'am, but I was just speaking out to you as if you were my sister!" Now it is just this motherly and sisterly influence which I want to see carried out into the social relations; and I am persuaded that something of the mother's authority and the sister's tenderness *does* sanctify every woman in the eyes of men where she is called upon and authorized to work out social good. All the ladies who went to the East bear uniform testimony to the excellent feeling of the poor men towards them. " Their submission and respect were quite filial, almost childlike," said one of these ladies with emotion.

These soldiers had probably no other idea of a *lady* than might be gained from a distant sight of their officers' wives, in riding habits, figuring at a review. The effect therefore which genuine ladyhood, dignified, quiet, refined, compassionate, produced on their minds when brought into daily intimate relation with them, was that mingled admiration and reverence, which the good of each sex ought to feel for the other, which the real lady will always inspire. These soldiers, we are told, could think and speak of nothing but " angels," just descended to earth, and would not have been much more astonished had these " angels " suddenly returned to Heaven through the roof or through the window. But the time will come when these things will excite as much

love and reverence, and less astonishment.
The same observations apply to the ministry
of ladies in a workhouse.*

I should say, from what I have seen, that it
is in the men's wards of the workhouses, and
yet more especially those of the boys, that
female supervision is required, and where lady
visitors would do essential good. Will they

* " The workhouse poor do sometimes see the more respectable portion of the male sex; the house is periodically visited
by the vestry; the rector occasionally goes round. There are
boards and board meetings, and before these the inmates are
allowed to prefer their complaints. But the best of the female
sex they *never* see. They do not know what ladies are, except
as they are spoken of as the mistresses of a house or the employers of servants. For the London workhouse poor, — I
speak of course within the limits of what I know, — belong
mainly to the class which has never come in contact with the
upper classes of society."

He speaks in another place of the "insensible influence
which the mere presence of ladies, their voice, their common
words, their ordinary manners, their thoughts, all that they
carry unconsciously about them, can exercise on the poor;
but this applies to real ladies, cultivated, gentle, well-born,
well-bred, not to vulgar, pretentious, meddling women calling
themselves *ladies*. ' There is no people more alive to gentle
blood and gentle manners than the English poor; ' and it is
not by undervaluing such distinctions, but making use of
them, that you will prevail." (See the whole of this Lecture
on Workhouse Visiting, the result of the Experience of a
Workhouse Chaplain. — *Lectures to Ladies*, p. 273 – 281.)

venture there? or will they think it "very improper?"

I was lately in a workhouse ward containing twenty-two beds; twenty-one were filled
with poor decrepit old women in the last
stage of existence. The nurse was, as usual,
a coarse old hag. In the twenty-second bed
was a young person of better habits, who had
been an invalid, but was not helpless; she
was there because she had no home to go to.
There was no shelf or drawer near her bed to
place anything in; this was not allowed, lest
spirits should be concealed. The book she was
reading, — anything she wished to keep for
herself, — was deposited in her bed, or under
it; nothing was done for comfort, and very
little for decency. The power of retiring for a
little space from all these eyes and tongues
was quite out of the question; and so it was
everywhere. A poor, decent old woman, sinking into death, in a ward where there were
twenty-five other inmates, wished to be read
to; but there was no one to do this. She
thought she would try to bribe one of the
others to read to her, by the offer of "a

hap'orth of snuff;" but even this would not do.*

I may not farther dwell upon details at present; but I would ask whether such a state of things could exist if some share in the administration and supervision of workhouses were in the hands of intelligent and refined women whose aid should be voluntary? Why should not our parish workhouses be so many training schools, where women might learn how to treat the sick and poor, and learn by experience something of the best means of administration and management?

I see that, in one of our large London parishes, (in a workhouse which, a few months ago, was conspicuous for the most disgraceful mismanagement, and held up to public indignation,) a committee of lady-visitors has been allowed to look over the wards. This will do good in individual cases; but what is wanted

---

* " It is the insolence of its officials, and the insubordination of its inmates, that make the poorhouse (what we have heard respectable paupers call it) *a hell upon earth*. It is intolerable that an asylum established by law, instead of being made formidable to the bad by the order it enforces, should be made revolting to the good by the license it permits." — *Quarterly Review*, Sept. 1855.

is a domestic, permanent, ever-present *influence*, not occasional *inspection*. It is, however, a step in the right direction. We must remember that lady-visitors, to do good, must be properly authorized and organized, — must work in concert, lest they contradict and interfere with each other. The bristling jealousy of sub-officials, must be soothed; the scruples about interfering with established powers have to be surmounted by sense, and kindness, and decision; there must be over all a supreme and harmonizing power; or the whole arrangement will fall asunder like ill-fitting bricks without cement. Of the possible mischief that may be done by ignorant, over-zealous, self-confident, excitable women, I shudder to think; and of the use that may be made of such failures to injure a good cause; yet were the experiment to fail twenty times over ere it succeed, it would never shake my conviction that the principle I advocate *must* be carried out at last; that it is God's law, by obedience to which we shall be saved; by neglect of which we perish.

I HAVE not found in my limited travels any institutions exactly similar to our workhouses, that is, charitable institutions supported by enforced contributions. There are, however, two institutions at Turin which struck me as very remarkable, and which may be said, each in its way, to fulfil some of the purposes for which our workhouses were original instituted.

One of these is a community of women called *Rosines*, from the name of their founder, Rosa Governo, who had been a servant girl. It cannot be styled a religious community, in the usual sense, as neither vows nor seclusion are required; it is a working joint-stock company, with a strong interfusion of the religious element, without which I believe it could not have held together. Here I found, wonderful to tell, nearly four hundred women of all ages, from fifteen and upwards, living together in a very extensive, clean, airy building (or rather assemblage of buildings, for they had added one house to another), maintaining themselves by their united labor, and carrying on a variety of occupations, as tailoring, embroidery (espe-

cially the embroidery of military accoutre-
ments for the army), weaving, spinning, shirt-
making, lace-making, — every thing, in short,
in which female ingenuity could be employed.
They have a large, well-kept garden; a school
for the poor children of the neighborhood; an
infirmary, including a ward for those whose
age had exempted them from work; a capital
dispensary, with a small medical library; here
I found one of the women preparing some
medicines, and another studying intently a
French medical work.

This female community is much respected
in Turin, and has flourished for more than a
century. It is entirely self-supported, and the
yearly revenue averages between 70,000 and
80,000 francs. The women are ruled by a
superior, elected from among themselves, and
in their workrooms were divided into classes,
or groups, each under direction of a monitress
to keep order. The rules of admission and
entrance and the interior regulations are strict.
Any inmate may leave at once whenever she
pleases, but (as I understood) cannot be re-
admitted. The costume, which is that worn

by the lower classes in 1740, when the community was founded, is not becoming, but not very peculiar. All looked clean and cheerful.

I have been assured by some of my friends, who ought to understand these matters, that such an institution would be "quite impossible" in England, because the education given to the girls of the working class renders it "quite-impossible" for a number of them to dwell together in unity, or in voluntary submission to a controlling power. If it be so, so much the worse! — but is it so?

The other institution I have alluded to, is yet more extraordinary, and of recent origin.

A few years ago a poor priest, who had served as chaplain in a hospital, being struck by the dreadful state of the convalescent women, who, after being dismissed as cured while yet too weak for labor, were obliged to have recourse to vice or to starve, fitted up a garret with four old half-rotten bedsteads, into which he received four wretched, sick, sinful creatures, and begged for their support. Such was the beginning of the "*Casa della divina Providenza*," called also "*La Casa Cotolengo*," from the name of its founder, who died about two years ago.

When I visited this extraordinary place, I found that the garret and its four old bedsteads had gradually extended to many ranges of buildings, for different purposes.* There is a hospital with two hundred beds; another hospital especially for wretched, diseased women out of the streets; another for children, containing fifty beds; a refuge for forsaken infants; a small school for deaf and dumb (children and others); a ward especially for epileptic patients and *crétins*. The attendance on this vast congregation of sick and suffering beings is voluntary, and considered by the physicians, nurses, and sisters as an act of religion. There were about two hundred attendants, men and women. The number of inmates constantly varied, and no regular account was kept of them: one day it was calculated to be about thirteen hundred, pa-

* The original " four old bedsteads " are preserved *in memoriam*, and were pointed out to me.

tients and nurses all included. The deaths are about six daily. All who would be rejected from other hospitals, who have incurable, horrid, chronic diseases, who are in the last stage of helpless, hopeless misery, come here; none are ever turned away. *There are no funds, and no accounts are kept;* nor, I must confess, is there any of the order and neatness of a regular hospital. All the citizens of Turin, more especially the poorer class, contribute something; and so "one day telleth another." "We trust to Divine Providence, and have hitherto wanted for nothing," was the reply to my inquiry. "Sometimes our coffer is empty, sometimes it is full. If we are poor to-day, we shall be richer to-morrow. God helps us!"

In England, a political economist or a poor-law commissioner would have been thrown into fits by such a spectacle of slovenly charity. Too true it is: —

"The wise want love, and they who love want wisdom;
  And all good things are thus confused to ill!"

AND now, having shown what an extensive field there is for work, what are the qualifications required in the workers? It is plain that mere kindly impulses and self-confidence (so different from practical benevolence and tender, humble faith!) will not suffice. By what means are we to prepare and discipline our women for the work they may be called to perform? What has been done, what may be done, to render them fitting helpmates for energetic and benevolent men, and instruments of beneficent power? These are momentous questions, which we have now to consider.

The complaint has become threadbare; yet I must begin by noticing the mere *fact* as such. There is no adequate provision for the practical education of the middle and lower classes of girls in this country; and (which is much worse) the importance of this want is either overlooked, or at least no one in power thinks it worth while to treat this part of educational statics with any particular attention. Open the books and pamphlets on national education, read the

speeches of our legislators, the clever leading
articles in our journals; everywhere it is
the same. The education of boys for professional and practical life, the sort of instruction which is to fit them for such and
such civil or military employments, are always
discussed as of the highest importance; and
the provision already made is, we are assured,
not nearly sufficient. What shall be said of
the general tone of feeling and opinion with
regard to the education of women? is it less
important than that of men? I will not go
into the extreme opinions of those who argue
that it is even *more* important, inasmuch as
women being the mothers of the human
race, a very large portion of their mental
and moral organization must pass into that
of their offspring. The saying of the wise
philosopher, " All our able men have had
able mothers," is, however, so generally true,
that the few exceptions only prove the rule.
Here I would merely suggest, that a sound
practical education preparatory to the duties
and business of real life is of as much importance to women as to men, and ought not

to be treated as comparatively insignificant, as merely accidental or accessory to the education of the other sex.* The tone of indifference assumed on this point, and the comparatively small means afforded, is a mistake for which we shall pay dearly.† It unites with other causes in lowering the standard of opinion in respect to women, besides being more directly injurious. I am

* In the year 1854, out of 159,727 marriages, 47,843 males and 68,175 females signed the marriage register by making their mark. In 1848, the proportion was the same : 43,166 males and 62,771 females were unable to write their names. So that the number of uneducated women is one third greater than the number of uneducated men. There remains, then, the astounding fact, that out of nearly 80,000 women who approached the altar, 68,175 could not write their names.

† The North British Review for June last, which I had not seen when this Lecture was written, contains an article entitled " Outrages on Women," already referred to (p. 161). In this excellent essay, the custom — must we call it so ? — of " wife-beating " is attributed not merely to ruffianism on the part of the man, but to the miserable, untidy, unhealthy dwellings of the poor, and the uncontrolled tempers, ignorance of what are called " common things," and want of all training in wifely and womanly duties and responsibilities, on the part of the women. If they have " aggravating tongues," and are unthrifty and untidy, having been taught no better, it is not a sufficient reason why they should be beaten, kicked, stamped upon; but it is a cause which should be taken into consideration by our legislators and educators.

acquainted with several of those ladies who had to select the hired nurses sent out to the East, and they could make terrible revelations on this subject. Out of the hundreds of women who offered themselves, it was scarcely possible to find a tenth of the number fit to be sent out; and more than the half of that number disgraced themselves, or were found useless when there. The ignorance, the incompetency, the slowness of the unexercised reasoning powers; the want of judgment and of thought which made it impossible for them to direct, the violent insubordinate tempers which made it impossible for them to obey, rendered them the plague of the authorities. Their degraded habits made them unfit to be trusted in the men's hospitals. They were drunken as well as dissolute, and the lady nurses felt themselves disgraced as Englishwomen and Christians in the eyes of the stranger and unbeliever. This was the case with two thirds of the hired nurses, and with almost all the soldiers' wives, very few of whom I believe were found available for any useful purpose. These women had all been in schools of one sort or another, — national schools, Sunday schools, — and this was the result.

Now I will tell you, as an illustration, what I have seen only very lately. I was in a very large parish union, where there were about four hundred children, nearly an equal number of boys and girls; and schools for both. The boys had an excellent master for reading and writing, and had masters besides, to teach them various trades. There was a tailor, a carpenter, a shoemaker, a hairdresser, a plumber, who, at wages from twenty-five to thirty-five shillings a week, were employed to instruct the boys in their respective trades. The girls were taught reading, writing, and sewing; some of them, under the pauper menials, helped to scour and scrub. The over-tasked, anxious mistress seemed to do her best; but there was not sufficient assistance. The whole system was defective and depress-ing, and could not by any possibility turn out efficient domestic servants, or well-disciplined, religious-minded, cheerful-tempered girls. I

was informed that, of the boys sent out of
this workhouse, about two per cent. returned
to the parish in want or unserviceable; while
of the girls they reckoned that about fifty per
cent. were returned to them ruined and depraved.* Remember, I do not give you this
as a general state of things in workhouse
schools, but merely as an illustration of the
prevalent opinion as to the sort of instruction

* On my repeating this official testimony to some friends of
mine, it was received with incredulous horror. I have since
found it fearfully corroborated by two other witnesses.

"Various metropolitan workhouses (St. George's, Hanover
Square, excepted) caused their refractory paupers to be committed to Cold Bath Fields, up to September, 1850, and we
witnessed in the demeanor of young girls, from twenty years
of age and upwards, such revolting specimens of workhouse
education, that the exhibition was at once frightful and disgusting. The inconceivable wickedness of those girls was
absolutely appalling." — (*Colonel Chesterton.*)

To this testimony from the governor of a prison I add that
of Mr. Brewer, chaplain of one of our great workhouses. He
says that the disorderly girls and boys in our streets " are
mainly the produce of the workhouse and the workhouse
schools. Over them society has no hold, because they have
been taught to feel that they have nothing in common with
their fellow men. *Their experience is not of a home or of
parents*, but of a workhouse and a governor, — of a prison and
a gaoler as hard and rigid as either." — (*Lectures to Ladies
on Practical Subjects*, p. 279.) Is this, then, one of the results
of our parish charities?

which is fitting and necessary for pauper
boys, compared with that which is thought
sufficient for pauper girls, and the result in
both cases.

The education given to many of our girls
of the higher, even the highest classes, is far
better calculated to turn out efficient working
women, than in those classes who are supposed to be born to labor. I think that in a
general way they are too well instructed in all
they have to avoid, and too little instructed in
all they have to do; still, where the tone of
the mind is raised by an acquaintance with
art and literature, where the intellect has been
exercised from childhood, where temper has
been restrained, at least from habitual good
manners, if not from higher motives, we have
something better to begin with than the low
principles, vacant minds, animal propensities,
and utter undisciplined tempers of the girls
who are intended for " service." But I am
glad to see that these evils are awakening
every day more and more attention.*

* See " Remarks on the Education of Girls," by Bessie
Rayner Parkes. Third edition.

It is a serious objection to present modes of
education in both sexes, that nothing is done
with the important aim of enabling them to
understand each other, and work together harmoniously and trustfully in after-life. There
seems, however, to exist among us an awakening and extending conviction that something
of this is necessary, and that the complete
separation of boys and girls in their early
education, while yet children, is a great mistake, and a source of infinite unhappiness and
immorality.* They are not accustomed to

---

* On this point I have spoken out elsewhere, and I repeat
it here. While children, — till eleven or twelve years old, at
least, — boys and girls ought to be accustomed to learn together, play together, eat together, to be mutually forbearing,
helpful, and kind to each other. More of the happiness and
morality of their after-life depends on their childish habits
than people would well believe. It was never contemplated,
by the natural law of domestic life, that the two halves of
humanity were created to be a mischief to each other. Such
was not God's design : " male and female created he them "
for wise and beneficent purposes. (Common-place Book,
2d edition, p. 217.) See also, on this point, the testimony of
an experienced schoolmaster, who has devoted a whole chap-
ter to the subject. ("Stow on the Training System ;" I
think, the sixth edition of that admirable and practical book.)
A friend writes to me : " We heard the idea highly commended
the other day by the master of the large Idiot school at Reigate.
He says the mixture of little boys and girls there has been of

each other, and when they are afterwards associated together in the labors of life, they have not been prepared for such communion by early childish habits of mutual dependence and mutual good will, such as the law of nature contemplated in domestic life, to which all education should as far as possible be assimilated. Thus, each sex herded together in separate schools, the faults of each are increased; and nothing is done in the system of teaching to supply by principle the incongruities of feeling and habits, and ignorance of each other, produced and fostered by this dreadful mistake; so when called upon to act in communion, unless bound together by some external conventional law, there is mutual restraint, mutual mistrust, if not a positive shrinking asunder; and this is a great evil in itself, and the cause of unnumbered evils in its social effects.

great service; and he mentioned one small instance of the good manners of the boys resulting from it, which from these poor creatures I thought was striking : ' When walking out two and two, of their own accord they formed into single file, politely making room for the girls to pass.' "

BUT suppose the necessity for a better and more sympathetic education for *all* conceded, and suppose it even already provided for by more enlightened public opinion, there remain some special and plausible objections against the training of women for active, and social, and responsible avocations, such as I have pointed out. Of these objections, which I have often had to listen to, three only appear to me worth a moment's attention.

And first, you hear people say, quite sententiously, " I object to anything which takes a woman out of her home, and removes her from the sphere of domestic duty." So do I! I object strongly to anything which takes a woman out of her proper sphere, out of a happy and congenial home, where her presence is delightful and her services necessary: *there* is her first duty. I object also to every thing which takes away a man from *his* first duty, the protection and support of his home. Let us bear in mind, that for every man who does not provide a home, there must exist a woman who must make or find a home for herself, somehow and somewhere. There

seems to be no objection to taking the lower
classes of women out of their homes to
be domestic servants, milliners, shop-women,
factory-girls, and the better educated to be
governesses. Then why should the objection
be urged, merely with respect to other employments, only because they are as yet
rather unusual, or at least not yet recognized
among us, but which are of a far more elevated kind?

Then there is much sentimental speech of
women being educated "to adorn a home," to
be a "good wife," "a good mother." And
how many women are there who have no
home, who are neither wives nor mothers, nor
never will be while they live? Will you deny
to them the power to carry into a wider
sphere the duties of home, — the wifely,
motherly, sisterly instincts, which bind them
to the other half of the human race? Must
these be utterly crushed; or may they not be
expanded and gratified healthily, innocently,
usefully? This, surely, is at least worth considering, before we allow the force of an

objection which seems to consist in phrases rather than in arguments.

A second objection, which I have heard chiefly from medical men, is, that the women of the educated classes, from which our volunteers are to be taken, are in general feeble, over-refined, and excitable, apt to take fancies to individuals where their aid and attention ought to be impartial and general, too self-confident for obedience, too sensitive to be trusted. That these objections apply to many women I have no doubt; that they apply to women generally I deny. Medical men have much more experience of the invalided and feeble portion of the sex, than of the healthful portion. They know the fatal influence which some of our conventional customs, and an ill understood physical education, have on the general health and development of girls. The sick fancies of idle, disappointed, desponding women give abundant occupation to clever physicians, who are satisfied to deal with the immediate physical

causes of disease, without troubling themselves with the antecedent and remote moral
causes; so it is very natural that they should
have great pity for us, but not much respect.
Few of them are sufficiently large minded
to perceive that the service of a better order of
women in our public institutions, by giving
employment to the unoccupied faculties and
feelings, would be a means of improved health
and cheerfulness not only in themselves but in
others, and that if women were trained and
prepared by a sufficient study and probation,
they would be made efficient and practical.

I have heard medical men, who were in
the Crimea, express their conviction that a
trial of English lady volunteer nurses *must*
end in total failure, and who at the same
time were loud and emphatic in their admiration of the Roman Catholic Sisters of
Charity. The objection then, apparently, is
not against women in general, but against
English women in particular, brought up in
the Protestant faith. Now, do they mean to
say that there is anything in the Roman
Catholic religion which produces these effi-

cient women? or that it is impossible to train any other women to perform the same duties with the same calm and quiet efficiency, the same zeal and devotion?. Really I do not see that feminine energy and efficiency belong to any one section of the great Christian community.

And now for the third objection; it is thus put: —

" Would you make charity a profession?"

Why not? why should not charity be a profession in our sex, just in so far (*and no farther*) as religion is a profession in yours! If a man attires himself in a black surplice, ascends a pulpit, and publicly preaches religion, are we, therefore, to suppose that his religious profession is merely a profession, instead of a holy, heartfelt vocation? If a woman puts on a grey gown, and openly takes upon herself the blessed duty of caring for the sick, the poor, the perverted, are we therefore to suppose that charity is with her merely a profession? Here we have surely a distinction without a difference! No doubt

we should all be religious, whether we assume
the outward garb or not; no doubt we should
all be charitable, whether in white, black, or
grey; but why should not charity assume
functions publicly recognized, — openly, yet
quietly and modestly exercised? Why is female influence always supposed to be secret,
underhand, exercised in some way which is
not to appear? — till even our good deeds
borrow the piquancy of intrigue, and we are
told practically to seek the shade, till morally
we fear the light? Why can we not walk
bravely, honestly, and serenely, yet simply and
humbly, along the path we have chosen, or to
which it hath pleased God to call us, instead
of creeping about in a spirit of fear, as if quite
overcome by the sense of our own wonderful
merits, and obliged to throw over them a veil
of conventional humility?

Our pretension to such avocations, as I have
mentioned, may possibly be met by just the
same arguments which fifty years ago were
launched against "literary ladies;" and if
sneers at "blue stockings," and female pedants

could have turned women from the cultivation of their minds, and crushed every manifestation of genius, no doubt it would have been done. Luckily, two admirable and gifted men, — Professor Playfair, with his profound science, and tender, generous feeling, and Sydney Smith, with all the force of his strong masculine sense, and all the splendor of his wit, — came to our rescue at a most critical period. The former claimed for us the department of science; the latter, that of literature and independent thought. This is twenty or thirty years ago. There are men now, equally manly and far-sighted, eager to instruct us and sustain us in well doing, eager to recognize in us fellow-laborers by divine appointment, companions by the grace of God, without whom no step in social progress can be attained, no lasting good achieved.

The commencement of a college for working women, the difficulties it has had to contend with, and its progress up to this time, are signal illustrations of the existence of the "great want" of which I have spoken, and the hopes and purposes which are filling thoughtful, active, beneficent minds. Shall I tell you what in this noble design has struck me with the deepest emotion, the deepest thankfulness? It is the interest with which men of the working class and professional men have received it. The former, when consulted, "spoke," Mr. Maurice says, "with remarkable freedom and intelligence: we gathered a great many more hints and opinions than we had at all expected." There were differences of opinion in respect to arrangements and details, but "entire unanimity on the main question. There was no indication whatever of the slightest fear that females should know as much as they themselves knew, or more than they knew. There was a manifest wish that they should have the same advantages. There was a distinct and positive call upon us, not to withhold from the one what we were trying to give to the other."

So far the intelligent working men. Even more fraught with encouragement and hope was the series of Lectures on practical subjects, addressed to a female audience, to educated women, who wished to know what it

was best for them to learn before they were
fitted to help and to teach. I was not present,
being abroad at the time; but, as I was informed, the audience collected was not so
large as might have been expected. That
was not surprising; but what was surprising,
and delightful too, there were found ready and
willing to deliver these lectures to ladies " on
practical subjects," eleven distinguished professional men; of these, six were clergymen,
three physicians, and two lawyers. The six
lectures delivered by clergymen dwelt of course
chiefly on the duty of well directed benevolence, in the hospital and in the workhouse,
in parish supervision, and district visiting: all
excellent in spirit and feeling. One, on the
" Teaching by Words," — capital, — as awakening the intellect to the uses and possible
abuses of language, as a key to thought as
well as an implement of thought. Perhaps, if
women were better taught the true value and
true significance of words, they would be the
less likely to pour them forth on light occasions.

The three lectures by the medical men are

all so excellent, that I felt lifted up in heart as
I closed the volume. The two lectures on
law, ("Law as it affects the Poor," and "Sanitary Law,") are useful and clear, though
technical.

It is not any where indicated in these lectures, that weakness and ignorance are to be
accounted as charms in women, by which
they are to recommend themselves to intelligent men; or that it is "unfeminine" to study
the conditions of health ; or that the desire
to know something of those divine laws,
" through which she lives, and moves, and
has her being," is the result of a " depraved
imagination ; " or that the wish to prepare
herself by experience to minister to disease
and affliction is to be sneered at as a " taste for
surgery." (I beg of you to observe that I am
here citing phrases which I have myself heard.)
Another spirit animates the writers of these
lectures.* Every where the important social

* See particularly the lecture on " The College and Hospital," and the lecture on " Dispensaries and allied Institutions," in which the importance, religious and practical,
attached to the study of physiology, is the same principle for
which the late Dr. Andrew Combe, and his brother Mr.
George Combe, have for years past contended.

work which rests on the woman is generally
acknowledged and wisely inculcated. She is
encouraged to think, and to carry out thought
into action.

The training of a better order of women
for hospital nurses is that department of social
usefulness which is more immediately before
the public, and it involves many considerations.

There is no question I have heard more
warmly contested, than the question of paid
or unpaid female officials. I think there
should be both. We should have them of
two classes; those who receive direct pay,
and those who do not. Consider the qualifications required. There must be force of
character of no common kind; the humility
which can obey, and the intelligence which
can rule; great enthusiasm, great self-com-
mand, great benevolence; quickness of perception with quietness of temper; the power
of dealing with the minds of others, and a
surrender of the whole being to the love and
service of God: without the religious spirit

we can do nothing. Now, can we hope to obtain these qualifications for any pay which our jails, workhouses, or hospitals could afford? — or indeed for any pay whatever? Yet it is precisely an order of women, quite beyond the reach of any remuneration that could be afforded, which is so imperatively required in our institutions.

The idea of service without pay seems quite shocking to some minds, quite unintelligible; they quote sententiously, " The laborer is worthy of his hire." True; but what shall be that hire ? Must it necessarily be in coin of the realm ? There are many women of small independent means, who would gladly serve their fellow-creatures, requiring nothing but the freedom and the means so to devote themselves. There are women who would prefer " laying up for themselves treasures in heaven," to coining their souls into pounds, shillings, and pence on earth; who having nothing, ask nothing but a subsistence secured to them; and for this are willing to give the best that is in them, and work out their lives while strength is given them. I believe that such service is especially blessed. I believe such service does not weary, is more gracious and long-suffering than any other, blessing those who give and those who receive. I believe it has a potency for good that no hired service can have.

The idea in this country that every thing has a money value, to be calculated to a farthing, according to the state of the market, is so ingrained into us, that the softest sympathies and highest duties, and dearest privileges of Christians, are never supposed to be attainable unless sold and paid for by the week, or month, or year. This is so much the case, that those who visit the poor people can hardly banish from their minds the conviction that there is some interested motive, some concealed, selfish object in doing so. Yet if once brought to believe that there is really only the wish for their good, how beautiful and how blessed becomes the intercourse! The two meanest forms of sensuality and selfishness in our lower classes, the love of money and the love of drink, are best combated by the combined religious and feminine influence. A

strong barrier to this vulgar greediness would
be produced, I think, by the presence and
employment of women officially authorized,
yet not hired, and doing their duty from pure
love of God and man.* It would give a
more elevated standard to many minds, to be
brought into relation with such women.

I find the admixture of voluntary and unpaid labor with hired labor, thus advocated in
an excellent article in the " Quarterly Review"
for September, 1855. " Many there doubtless
are, who, without neglecting duty, may engage
in this office of charity, and thus shun the
dangers of the world they dread, or find a
refuge from the hardness of a world which has

---

* " The profound consolation which one derives from the
remembrance of Miss Nightingale's services in the war is that
they entirely confound the notion that only paid jobs are done
effectually; that work undertaken from love must be performed in a slovenly, unbusiness-like way. That has been
the conviction of our English public; it has been put again
and again into solemn maxims; and all acts not assuming
them for their foundation have been laughed to scorn. Miss
Nightingale has turned the laugh in the other direction.
There has been slovenliness enough in many departments.
The tasks that have been done most thoroughly have been
done from a divine inspiration." — *Lectures to Ladies on
Practical Subjects*, p. 17.

lost its power to please though not to wound them; and thus far at least is clear, that whether they sacrifice its pleasures, or seek a shelter from its vexations, their presence at the sick-bed will diffuse the zeal of love and the charm of refinement over an office which has hitherto, at the best, been executed with the cold regularity of routine."

But to render the hired labor efficient and reliable, it must be placed at the disposal of the voluntary and unpaid labor, and be in all respects subordinate; as is the case in King's College Hospital. The want of this regulation produced some mischief in the East, which I shall have to revert to further on.

Then, as to whether the women who devote themselves to these services should or should not be associated into a community, is a question hotly debated, to be settled I think by the individual vocation.

One says, " I cannot work with other people; I must go on in my own way." Well, let her go on in her own way, let her go on working single-handed as is good in her own

eyes; and God forbid that I should under-
value the good done simply and religiously by
some excellent women I know working in
their own way! But another says, " I feel the
need of a bond of sympathy; it strengthens
and sustains me. I should like to have my
work cut out and appointed for me, and to
labor in association both with men and women." And this is well also. There is room,
there is work, for both. I think a community
might be formed on a broader principle than
that which is contemplated, I believe, by the
council of the Nightingale fund, for the mere
preparation of hospital nurses; but am too
well aware of the difficulties from within and
without not to hail a beginning, though it fall
far short of that which is required; only we
must keep our eyes fixed on the larger views.

Where the objects are of great importance,
and have to do with our own deepest, inner-
most life, it requires an especial training of
the mind and habits to preserve, in the subjection of the individual will, all the freshness
and energy of the mental powers. To resign
the highest privileges of individual action,

and yet preserve the highest privileges of the individual conscience, this may be difficult, but it has been proved not to be impossible. But, I repeat, the individual inclinations and gifts must settle this.

I am sure that my Roman Catholic friends are sincere in their belief that such a community can take root and succeed only in their Church. At all events, it is the interest of the Roman Catholic priesthood to persuade us that the power of working a public charitable institution by a due admixture of the religious and feminine element with the masculine directing will, belongs to them only. This is very natural on their part, and wise, and quite intelligible; but is it wise of our most influential clergymen to play into their hands, to act and preach as if this plea were true? As if this privilege of the woman to pervade our human institutions with a more tender and more moral power, to work openly with a species of religious sanction, like the Deaconesses of the primitive Christian Church, were really and inseparably interwoven with the doctrines of the Roman Catholic Church, so that we cannot have Sisters of Charity without accepting also an infallible pope, transubstantiation, the immaculate conception, and Heaven knows what besides, the terror and abomination of our evangelicals? Surely it is an injury to the cause of religious freedom and human progress, an insult to their own peculiar form of faith, for any sect to acknowledge that what they allow to be good and desirable, and even necessary in itself, is inextricable from what they believe to be false and ensnaring. These views are every day driving distinguished, and gifted, and enthusiastic women, into the pale of that Church, which stretches out its arms, and says, " Come unto me, ye who are troubled, ye who are idle, and I will give you rest and work, and, with these, sympathy, and reverence, the religious sanction, direction, and control!" Can we find nothing of all this for our women? Why should they thus go out from among us? I, for my part, do not understand it.

In England it is not the form of Christiani-

ty we profess which is against such an organization of feminine aid in good works as I
would advocate ; — God forbid! Yet some
of our greatest difficulties may be ascribed
to the deep-rooted puritanic prejudices be-
queathed to us by our ancestors. It is worth
considering that the first effect of the Calvin-
istic reaction against the dominant Church,
and against the errors, and exaggerations, and
gross materialism which had been connected
with the worship of the Virgin Mother, was
not favorable to women. In the earlier times
of the Christian Church, whenever certain
women distinguished themselves by particular
sanctity or charity, or exercised any especial
moral or intellectual influence, the Church
absorbed them, claimed them, held them up
to reverence during life, and canonized them
after death; and still their beautiful images
shine upon us from our cathedral windows,
or stand out in sculptured forms in all the
dignity of their hallowed office and venerable
religious attributes. But after these fair superstitions had been abrogated by the severity
of the early reformers, and were succeeded by

the strongest prejudice against women exercising any kind of open and authorized religious or spiritual influence, still there were
women who did exercise such influence, —
the natural power of strong intellect, or strong
enthusiasm. The superiority could not be
denied; but as it could no longer be referred
to a larger measure of heavenly gifts, it must
be derived from demoniac power. Men had
repudiated angels and saints, but they still
devoutly believed in devils and witches. The
benign miracles of female charity were the
inventions and impositions of a lying priesthood; but woe unto him who doubted in the
power of an old woman to ride on a broom-
stick, or of a young woman to entertain Satan
as her emissary in mischief! All the women
who perished by judicial condemnation for
heresy in the days of the inquisition did not
equal the number of women condemned ju-
dicially as witches, — hanged, tortured, burned,
drowned like mad dogs, — in the first century
of the Reformed Church; and these horrors
were enacted in the most civilized countries
in Europe, by grave magistrates and ecclesi-

astics, who were proud of having thrown off the Roman yoke, and of reading their Bibles, where apparently they found as many texts in favor of burning witches as ever did the Inquisitors in favor of burning heretics. It was characteristic of the two diverging superstitions, that in the former age Dante conceived his Beatrice as the type of loving, wise, and spiritual womanhood, leading her lover into Paradise; while Milton's type of female attraction was Eve, the temptress to sin and death. The time is come, let us hope, when men have found out what we may truly be to them, not worshipping us as saints, or apostrophizing us as angels, or persecuting us as witches, or crushing us as slaves; revering us for that power we are allowed to possess, not jealous of it, nor throwing it into some indirect or unhealthy form; profiting by our tenderness, not oppressing us because of it; taking us to themselves as helpers in all social good, not leaving our undirected energies to wear away our own lives, and sometimes trouble theirs.

It is better than a dozen sermons on toleration, to count up the women who, during this half-century, have left the strongest and most durable impress on society, — on the minds and the hearts of their generation. First, there is Mrs. Fry, the Quakeress, to whom we owe the cleansing of our prisons, and in part the reform of our criminal code; Caroline Chisholm, the Roman Catholic, with her strong common sense, her decision and independence of character, who may be said to have reformed the system of emigration; Mary Carpenter, the Dissenter, who has become an authority in all that concerns the treatment of juvenile delinquents; and Florence Nightingale, the Churchwoman, who in our time has opened a new path for female charity and female energy. And let us remember that there is not one of these four admirable women who has not been assailed in turn by the bitterest animosity, by the most vulgar, so-called religious abuse from those who differed from them in their religious tenets, or from those who contemned them, and would have put them down merely as women; not one of them who has not outlived prejudice and jealousy; not one of them who could have carried out their large and beneficent views without the aid of generous and enlightened men, — men who had the nobleness of mind to accept them as fellow-workers in the cause of humanity, to admit them on equal terms into the communion of labor and the communion of charity.

WHEN I was abroad last year, I was led to make inquiries into that system of training which had been found so successful in turning out efficient, healthful, cheerful, kindly women. I found that it varied in the different communities, according to the different rules and objects of each; but in general these are the principal things attended to.

In the first place, none are accepted, even as probationers, who are of a sickly or weak organization.

Every one who is accepted brings a small sum of money in her hand, at least 500

francs, that is, from about thirty to forty
pounds. It is argued, that if a woman be
at all respectable, and not driven to take up
a religious and charitable vocation from mere
want, she must have friends, or find friends,
to subscribe for her this small dowry. In
the Order of Charity of Vincent de Paul,
none are accepted who have filled any servile office whatever, even that of a femme-
de-chambre. On my exclaiming against this
rule as frequently shutting out women already
to a certain degree efficient and experienced,
my informant answered, " Yes, but it has
been found by experience that those who
have been accustomed to sell their services
for a certain hire, become so imbued by this
habit, or notion, or feeling, that it is impossible to trust them, or to place confidence
in the higher principle which may appear
to have actuated them." " No doubt," she
added, " there may be exceptions, honorable
exceptions; but we are obliged to adhere to
a general rule, the wisdom of which has
been justified by two centuries of experience."
After a probation of six months, none are re-

tained in the society whose vocation appears
weak or uncertain, or who shrink from the
duties imposed upon them as painful or difficult. Everywhere I observed that exceeding
care is taken to adapt the especial work to
the individual nature ; a woman, for instance,
who excels in care and sympathy for children,
does not always make a good sick-nurse;
and some women who do not nurse their
own sex well, are found admirably efficient
and patient in the men's wards, and in the
military hospitals. Some have a talent for
managing the insane, and are instructed accordingly. Some who have a particularly
tender, enthusiastic, and cheerful temperament, are found excellent attendants for the
very aged and incurably infirm. Thus they
do not clash among themselves, nor does
each fancy herself fitted for something different from what she is set to do. This
discernment in the selection of fit instruments, this careful adaptation of the work
to the natural tendencies, this apportioning
of the labor to the mental and physical
strength, is, I am sure, one cause of that

cheerfulness and harmony of spirit, that serene and healthy look, which we observe in these Sisters of Charity, and which reacts in so remarkable a manner on the minds and the nerves of those to whom they minister. I should add, that those who manage the dispensaries receive a regular medical training, under an experienced apothecary.

In the East, when many of our volunteer ladies were ill or "knocked up," and obliged to return home; when the hired nurses were either ill or useless through their ignorance, disobedience, or immorality, and dismissed in disgrace, the well-trained Sisters of Charity or of Mercy held on with unflagging spirit and energy, never surprised, never put out, ready in resource, meeting all difficulties with a cheerful spirit; a superiority which they owed to their previous training and experience, not certainly to any want of zeal, benevolence, or intelligence in their Protestant Sisters of the better class.

I suppose it is well known that they are never paid wages, but a certain sum is paid by the hospital, or prison, or the family who employ them, to the house or community they belong to. The lowest sum is about 12*l.* a year, and they are besides provided with food and clothing. Those Sisters who have a high reputation for skill and experience are rated at a higher sum; and though they do not personally derive any profit from it, they have, I am told, a just pride in the higher value placed on their services.*

* I have been told of a French Sister of Charity who, for many years, attended a certain division of the French army in every campaign. On the field of battle, her energy, her presence of mind, had saved many lives, and she obtained such an influence over the men as rendered her an object of deep respect to them and to their officers. According to the rule of her order, she had made no distinction on the field of battle between friends and enemies, or rather none were enemies; and she had received from the military authorities of Austria, Prussia, and Russia crosses of merit, in acknowledgment of the lives she had saved. After the war was over, she retired from age and infirmity to the shelter of her convent; but she was allowed to wear these decorations over her religious habit, as it appeared to give her pleasure, perhaps as much pleasure as a star or a medal might give a valiant soldier. From her own people she could, of course, receive no reward whatever, it would have been against all rule; but they found a recompense for her, which seems to me very appropriate, very touching. The minister of war conferred on her the privilege of pardoning in every year two soldiers condemned to death; and so long as she lived she exercised this privilege. She died, I believe, about four or five years ago.

How far these rules and regulations may be found applicable among ourselves, must be a matter of consideration and experiment. I am inclined to think that many of them might be adopted, if once those unreal spectral difficulties, which strike terror into superstitious minds, could be surmounted.

For instance, in matters of dress we are in this country too apt to consider the adoption of any particular costume as popish and fantastical; that is to say, we admit the despotism of fashion, we rebel against the suggestion of reason; we profess a boundless submission to the French milliners, wear modes of dress against which good taste, convenience, even our purses and our sense of propriety revolt; we protest against them, but dare not walk the street except in a bonnet the most odious, the most unbecoming, the most garish, the most unfeminine, that insane fantasy ever invented. Meantime, if a dress be contrived to meet the requirements and proprieties of a certain vocation, unobtrusive, close-fitting, commodious, seemly, we rebel against it, we

repudiate any interference with our individual
liberty, individual caprice, and individual
bad taste. We forget that the dress has its
morale, — that if it be capable of affecting the
imagination through the senses in a draw-
ing-room, it will have the same power in a
sick-room, and that it ought not to be left
in the power of ignorance, or vulgarity, or
thoughtlessness, to do through trifling means
a real mischief.

Lately, in walking through the sick wards
of a workhouse, I spoke to two hired nurses,
who had been sent from our great hospitals
to superintend and train the pauper nurses
(a recent innovation, by the way, and one of
excellent promise). One of these women
wore a washed-out chintz gown of gay colors,
a dirty pink ribbon with a gilt gaudy brooch
about her neck; and on her head a very dirty
cap, with dangling white beads. The other
woman was in similar attire, except that her
very dirty cap was decorated with faded, dirty,
artificial flowers. In both cases the attire
had all the appearance of having come out
of a second-hand frippery shop; in both cases

the desire was the same, to be distinguished
from the pauper nurses, who wore the always
odious workhouse dress: therefore, these respectable women flaunted in the habiliments
of a street-walker.

If a physician came to prescribe for our
sick or dying friend in the dress of a fast
Oxonian dandy, or a sporting flash man,
should we approve of it? Yet here is the
same direct violation of decency and good
feeling. I contend that this is not right;
that there is a fitness in things which those
who do not intuitively appreciate should be
taught.

The genuine horror of a community of
women associated for religious and charitable
purposes entertained by some most excellent
people, who are accustomed to see things
only on one side and *from* one side, is hardly
conceivable by those who have looked into
the working of such communities; for instance, I find, in a very charming little book,
the following passage of eloquent objurga-
tion : —

" Look out," says the writer, " a clever, enthusiastic woman, with a strong will of her own, and no stronger will to control it; make her the Lady Superior of a sisterhood, without any man to come, with a weight of years, authority and holiness, to say to her, *this* must not be, — *that* would be very silly, or unreasonable, or improper, and I positively forbid it: * — do this, and you will do the devil's work in frustrating a means of good as effectually as himself could do. You will get sisterhoods in all the slavish misery of nuns, and with none of the protection of convents, — a pack of unhappy women, forbidden to exercise common sense, and rendered morbid, sensitive, and undevout by the system which the uncontrolled power of the Lady Superior exercises over them; and not rarely you will have the Lady Superior go crazy, because of the unlimited indulgence of

---

* Hence we are to infer that it is a reproach to a Protestant Sisterhood that they are emancipated from such control ; while one of the strongest objections made to the Roman Catholic Sisters of Charity is, that they are under the control and dictation of the priests.

her talent for government." * Of course, if
you *do this*, if you build with bad materials,
your edifice will be crazy. But why take it
for granted that your material is to be bad,
or that the devil is of necessity to interfere?
Now, over against this gratuitous picture of a
sisterhood, let us place another of a brother-
hood by way of pendant.

Take a house intended by Christians to
be an asylum for the poor; fill it with some
hundreds of the ruined, the reckless, the depraved; the aged, the helpless, the homeless;
with wailing infants, with unwed mothers,
and all the infinite grades of sin and suffering.
Bring this mass of human agonies together;
cram them close in horrid propinquity, in
filth, and fetid air, — the evil to deprave the
good, the better-educated where curses and
the foulest language pollute their ears; place
this institution, — this Christian, charitable
institution,— under the government of a set of
men, armed with a grim authority, called, as
if in mockery, "guardians of the poor;" let

* The Owlet.

there be no woman near them, to whisper
" *this* is wrong," or " *that* is cruel and unreasonable, and in the name of a God of mercy
I forbid it;" let there be no cheerful, genial
influence there, no gentle voice nor light
tread, but drunken viragoes to nurse the sick,
and insolent officials to feed the hungry : do
this, and you will have something as near
as possible to what we can conceive of an
earthly Hell, — you will have an ill-managed
Parish Workhouse.

But why picture as necessary and inevitable extremes which we may hope are only
accidental? Why imagine a "pack of women " on one hand, and a " pack of men " on
the other? Suppose we were to try what
might be the effect of neutralizing the mobility,
sensibility, and excitability of the women by
the firmness and judgment of the men?
Would not that be better?

I MUST now conclude with a few last words.

We cannot look around us without seeing that a demand has not only been created, but becomes every day increasingly urgent, for a supply of working women at once more efficient and more effective. I use the words advisedly as distinct in meaning; women and men too are *efficient* through energy and experience, and *effective* through higher gifts and sympathies, — higher aims and motives; *materially* efficient, *morally* effective. Meantime, with no want of zeal or aptitude, there is such a lamentable deficiency in training, in knowledge, in the means or opportunity of acquiring either, that I should despair, — if I were not too old to despair, — if I had not so often counted up the price we have to pay for truth, and the penance we must pay for falsehood too. If, among the hapless women I see struggling to bring their external existence into harmony with their inner life, — or what is harder still, to bring their inner life into subjection to harsh and deteriorating circumstance, — one half should go distracted, and

the other half turn Roman Catholics, I might
" even die with pity ; " but certainly not yield
up one inch of the ground I have taken, nor
one iota of the faith that is in me.

I remember that, when speaking on these
subjects to a very benevolent and accomplished
man, a clergyman, he said thoughtfully : " I
have little doubt that you are right ; and yet
if there be such a divine law involving all
human well-being and progress in its recognition, — how is it that it has not been more
distinctly revealed to us ? how is it that it
comes to us now like a novelty to be sub-
jected to the examination of the sceptical and
the carping of the foolish ? "

I did not answer.

We know that there has existed from the
commencement of the creation a law of God,
binding the whole universe into one harmoni-
ous whole, guiding the planets in their orbits,
connecting our own world with far-off worlds
of light and life, and at the same time so
regulating our least movements on this earth,
that we cannot put one foot before the other,
but in subjection to it. Yet of the existence

of this law we knew nothing, till, one hundred
and fifty years ago, the fall of an apple revealed it to Newton; and to what revelations
most important to our well-being has it not
since led! And may there not be a law of
moral and physical life as universal, as essential, as eternal, which in its agency has always
been felt, and yet in its relation to happiness
and progress, is only just beginning to be
understood, and not yet fully applied? I
do not say it *is* so; but may it not possibly
be so?

In general there is among men, — superior
men, — a strong, generous sympathy with the
cause I advocate. How noble and good I
have found them! how raised in their manly
power above all vulgar masculine jealousies!
Yet some among them, some *practical* men so
called, who start at shadows, — some members
of parliament who weigh truth and expediency
against each other in their political balance,
— some clergymen, bending down from the
height of their white neckcloths, half-sympa-
thizing, half-patronizing, — these say to me,

" We really cannot deal with abstract principles, we must work with such material as
we have at hand. What is your plan? If
we knew what plan you have formed we
might help you. What do you propose to
do ? "

I must confess I have no plan ready prepared, and so exquisitely contrived to avoid
offence that, like a mill-wheel with all the cogs
shaved off that it may work smoothly, it will
impart no movement, and do neither good nor
harm. But if there be vitality in the principle
I have placed before you, — the communion
of love and of labor, — then that which springs
out of it will be vital too, not working like a
machine, but bearing fruit like the tree.

And " what would I *do?* " they ask. Nothing more can I do indeed, but that which I
am now doing, or rather trying to do, with
such small power as God has given me.

I would place before you, this once more,
ere I turn to other duties, that most indispensable yet hardly acknowledged truth, that
at the core of all social reformation, as a
necessary condition of health and permanency

in all human institutions, lies the working of
the man and the woman together, in mutual
trust, love, and reverence.

I would impress it now for the last time on
the hearts and the consciences of those who
hear me, that there is an essential, eternal law
of life, affirmed and developed by the teaching
of Christ, which if you do not take into
account, your fine social machinery, however
ingeniously and plausibly contrived, will at
last fall into corruption and ruin. Wherever
men and women do not work together help-
fully and harmoniously in accordance with
the domestic relations, — wherever there is
not THE COMMUNION OF LOVE AND THE COM-
MUNION OF LABOR, — there must necessarily
enter the elements of discord and decay.

Despair we cannot, dare not.

If men bring their conventionalities and
practicabilities into conflict with the natural
law of God's divine appointment, we know
which must in the end succumb. Meantime
I would, if possible, assist in diminishing
the duration and the pain of that conflict.

If any thing I have now spoken carry conviction into the kind hearts around me, help! those who can and will, — and God help us all!

THE END.